The Product-Led Playbook

How to Unlock Self-Serve Revenue and Dominate Your Market (With a Tiny Team)

By Wes Bush

ProductLed.com

Portions of several chapters have appeared previously as blog posts.

Book cover by Missy Boscay.

Illustrations and templates by Missy Boscay.

1st edition, 2024.

Praise from Product-Led Founders

"Buy back your time by reading this book—it'll save you from making countless rookie mistakes when scaling a product-led business."

– Dan Martell, Wall Street Journal bestselling author of Buy Back Your Time

"We took Userflow from $0 to $5M ARR with just three employees. This book is the go-to manual for building a successful product-led business like ours."

– Esben Friis-Jensen, Co-Founder of Userflow

"*The Product-Led Playbook* offers a vital lesson that we learned firsthand at Vidyard: treating product-led growth as just a product initiative rather than a company-wide strategy is a recipe for failure. Wes' insights on organizational alignment are spot on and essential for any company serious about PLG success."

– Michael Litt, CEO of Vidyard

"Implementing the ProductLed System has been a game-changer for Groove. The only way to bootstrap a SaaS from $0 to $10M ARR in three years with 50%+ profit margins and a tiny team is by becoming product-led! Wes' insights and strategies are invaluable for any business looking to grow the smart way."

– Alex Turnbull, CEO and Founder of GrooveHQ and Helply

"There's only one way to build a $40M+ ARR, bootstrapped SaaS company without a large sales team—you must become product-led. This book shows you exactly how to do it."

– Nathan Barry, Founder and CEO at ConvertKit

"Being product-led is critical to running a profitable SaaS business. It's how we went from $0 to $26M in six years, bootstrapped. It's the guide I wish I had when I started—and now it's yours."

– Guillaume Moubeche, Founder and CEO at Lempire

"The first book by Wes Bush became mandatory onboarding reading for every new employee joining Omnisend. The product-led growth approach helped us bootstrap to $50M ARR and continues to be at the core of our growth philosophy. *The Product-Led Playbook* is a must-read for every company looking to become the obvious choice in their market while maintaining high efficiency."

– Rytis Lauris, Co-founder and CEO at Omnisend

"From day one, OpenPhone's product-led approach has been a game-changer, setting us apart in a market full of clunky business phone options. As more companies realize that customers demand a simple experience, being product-led will become the standard. *The Product-Led Playbook* is your invitation to disrupt your market, just as we have."

– Daryna Kulya, Co-founder at OpenPhone

"Wes' no BS approach to scaling a product-led business works—it helped us double our paying customers using the same marketing efforts. *The Product-Led Playbook* is packed with practical tips, templates, and guidance to help your product sell itself. If you're serious about growth, every minute you're not reading this book is a missed opportunity."

– Will Royall, Founder and CEO at PromoTix

"I can confidently say that this book is a masterclass in product-led growth. It's the blueprint for anyone serious about building a sustainable and impactful SaaS company."

– Liam Martin, Co-founder at Time Doctor and Running Remote, WSJ Bestselling Author

"Wes has unlocked a predictable process for product-led growth that empowers any business to scale purposefully, profitably, and powerfully by leveraging your product. Read this before your competition does."

– Jonathan "JCRON" Cronstedt, former President at Kajabi

"We built a $100M business the hard way… without product-led growth. I wish Wes' book had been written a decade ago. Get your hands on this book and learn how to conquer the chaos and build a scalable SaaS business the product-led way."

– Clate Mask, Co-Founder and CEO at Keap and author of Conquer the Chaos

"This playbook is a non-negotiable read for every founder and their team—every single year, no excuses. It's loaded with no-nonsense, actionable advice that's impossible to argue with. We've been building a profitable product-led company for over a decade, and this playbook lays out everything you need to know—trust me!"

– Bridget Harris, Co-Founder and CEO at YouCanBookMe

"We will turn RB2B into a $1B company (with less than 10 employees). The ONLY way to do that is by becoming product-led. This book shows you how."

– Adam Robinson, Founder and CEO at Retention and RB2B

"As a product person who's built a profitable business through a product-led approach for years, I can confidently say that having this resource from the start would have made the journey much smoother. Wes has crafted a comprehensive guide packed with insights and practical frameworks to take your product to the next level."

– Mert Alican Bektaş, founding team member and Head of Product at UserGuiding

"If you're a founder of a product-led business, this book is a must-read. Our team has helped 1,500 tech founders successfully sell their businesses, and this playbook outlines the best practices and actionable steps to position your business for higher multiples."

– Thomas Smale, CEO at FE International

"We've acquired 16 product-led SaaS companies ($50M+ in collective ARR), and I can say that *The Product-Led Playbook* is the definitive guide for creating a scalable, profitable product-led business."

– Dirk Sahlmer, Head of Origination at SaaS.Group

THE PRODUCTLED LIBRARY

The Complete Toolkit to Mastering Product-Led Growth

No matter where you are in your journey, there's a book for you and your team. Unlock the full potential of your product—starting now.

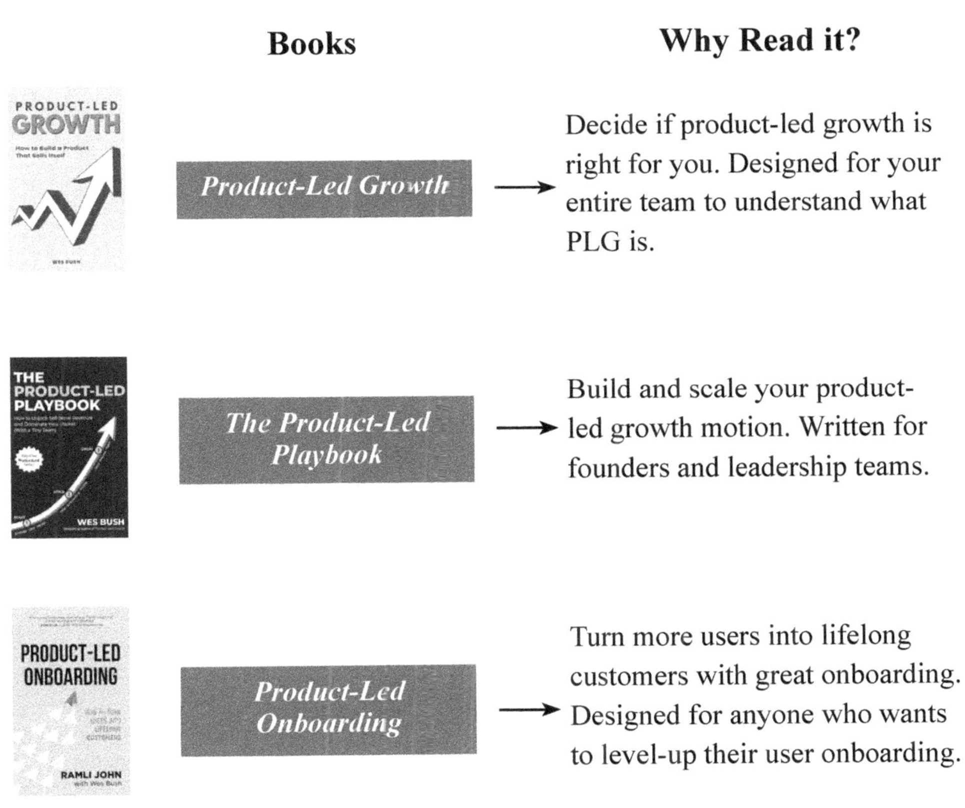

Books
Why Read it?
Product-Led Growth
Decide if product-led growth is right for you. Designed for your entire team to understand what PLG is.
The Product-Led Playbook
Build and scale your product-led growth motion. Written for founders and leadership teams.
Product-Led Onboarding
Turn more users into lifelong customers with great onboarding. Designed for anyone who wants to level-up their user onboarding.

Visit www.productled.com to get everything you need to fully implement the ProductLed System in your company today.

I built this playbook to help our clients master product-led growth. After witnessing its transformative impact, I knew it had to be shared with a wider audience. Product-led companies—where the product itself drives acquisition, retention, and expansion—are a force for good, democratizing access by making things cheaper, faster, and more accessible. But let's be real—building a product-led business isn't easy. This book is for those with the guts to take on the challenge. It's your playbook for building and scaling a product-led business that truly makes a difference.

Table of Contents

Introduction

The Product-Led Playbook

What This Book Is, How It Can Help You, and Who I Am

Right now, the survival rate for product-led companies is shockingly low, with most failing to sustain themselves.

A new, more reliable playbook is required. I am guessing that's why you're reading this book.

This book exists for two reasons:

1. **To Scale Your Business:** My primary goal is to help your product-led business thrive as quickly as possible so you can validate that my playbook works.
2. **To Partner for Greater Impact:** Once you've seen the results for yourself, I want to partner with ambitious SaaS founders like you—companies I believe have the potential to become the obvious choice in their market.

We're building a portfolio of product-led companies poised to become the obvious choice in their markets, and we want you to be a part of it.

This is not a book about why you should become product-led. If you're not convinced product-led growth (PLG) is right for you, read my bestselling book *Product-Led Growth: How to Build a Product That Sells Itself.*

This book is for ambitious SaaS founders and their go-to-market (GTM) teams who want to build a multi-million dollar business with a lean team. Simply telling companies to be like Slack, Zoom, or Canva isn't actionable. This is the no-BS manual on how to actually *do* it.

What follows is a practical, 9-part system that will change the way you scale a product-led business, and perhaps the way you *do* business, forever.

At ProductLed, we help SaaS companies transition from winging it with PLG to scaling every year. Since 2017, we've helped 400+ SaaS companies generate over $1B+ in self-serve revenue.

This system will work for you if you have a solid product, some customers, and solve a meaningful problem in the market. Please don't read this book if you don't have customers yet.

Although a product-led motion will help you get more customers in a scalable way, you need to start by talking to potential customers before rolling it out. Don't skip customer development.

As Steve Blank, the Pioneer of Customer Development, would say, "Cheating on customer development is like cheating on your parachute-packing class." It's not worth it.

To get the most out of this book, do three things:

1. Implement what you learn—this is a playbook, after all.
2. Share this book with your team to go through the activities together.
3. Follow the order outlined. Scaling has a strategic order.

There's also one pinnacle disclaimer: *You have to do the work to get the results.*

Why Trust Me As Your Guide

There's a mountain of content on PLG—some good, most confusing. Here's why you should choose me:

Trailblazing PLG Pioneer

I've made many mistakes building and scaling product-led businesses (just wait for the next chapter), and I share these lessons openly. As the author of *Product-Led Growth: How to Build a Product That Sells Itself*, a book read by over 500,000 people, I have established myself as the leading expert in PLG. I'm naturally a trailblazer, constantly pushing the boundaries and staying at the forefront of PLG trends—keeping you ahead of the curve.

Holistic, Practical Approach

I simplify complex concepts into bite-sized, actionable frameworks. Just ask any of my clients. This holistic PLG approach covers every aspect of your business, from onboarding to pricing. I provide actionable advice that can be implemented immediately, making PLG accessible and achievable for businesses of all sizes. Plus, as a founder, I know how tough building a product-led business can be, and I share only proven strategies.

Proven Results

Whether you're new to PLG or scaling it further, this proven system has consistently driven success for companies at every stage of their journey:

- **Boomi**: This $4 billion company doubled its free-to-paid conversion rate after transitioning to PLG and now gets 10% of its customers from a self-serve motion.
- **Keap**: This $100M ARR company tightened its product-led strategy and significantly improved its free-to-paid conversion rates.
- **Enzuzo**: This small team of three relaunched its freemium model and doubled its conversion rate within six months.

PLG works. But it's not a magic bullet.

Why PLG Is Only Half the Story—and What to Do About It

In 2015, Forrester conducted a groundbreaking study on B2B buyer preferences.[1] They asked a straightforward question: "Do you prefer talking to a salesperson or self-educating?"

Three out of four preferred to self-educate.

That was eight years ago. Have buyer preferences evolved? In 2024, ProductLed ran a survey with an even simpler question: "How do you prefer to buy?"

The options were:

1. Try before you buy.
2. Talk to someone in sales.

Only 3% of buyers preferred speaking to sales, while a whopping 97% wanted to try before buying. This is a seismic shift, not a trend.[2]

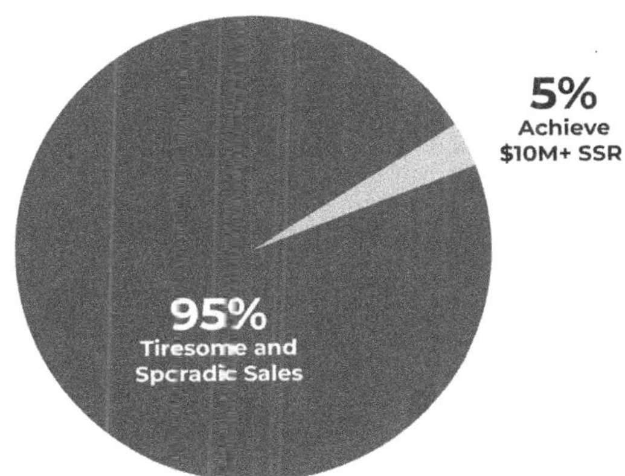

*As of August 27, 2024

*Source: ProductLed Index, based on data collected from 2043 SaaS businesses from 2023-2024.

Most users in your market want to try before they buy, too.

Yet, when we analyzed 568 B2B SaaS homepages for their primary call-to-action (CTA), here's what we found:

1. Demo only – 50%
2. Try before you buy only – 28%
3. Hybrid (has both a demo and try-before-you-buy option) – 22%

Fifty percent of SaaS companies are still sales-led. There's a massive delta between what buyers want and what SaaS companies offer.

If you want to sell to a modern buyer, you *must* have a try-before-you-buy experience—and it's got to be great.

Of the companies offering it, only 7% of users say it's a great experience.[3]

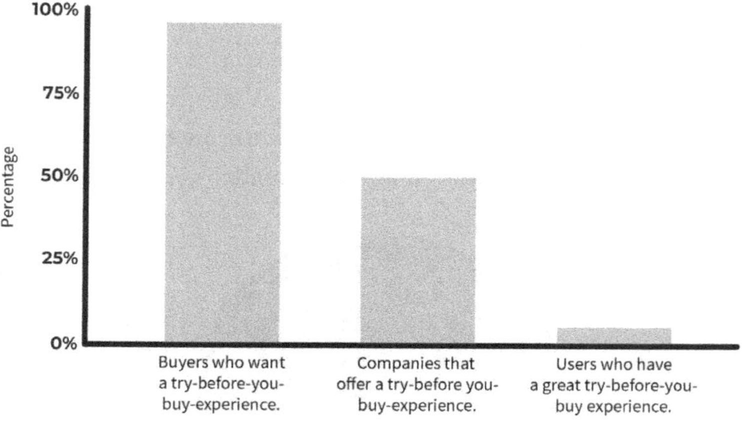

Based on data collected from LinkedIn in July 2024.

So why doesn't every company just launch one, given the low bar? Or why don't the 93% of companies with a mediocre try-before-you-buy experience optimize it?

Because building a product-led business is hard.

Why do so few companies excel with PLG? Why do most struggle to achieve meaningful scale despite overwhelming customer demand? That is the (multi) million-dollar question we'll unpack throughout this book.

The companies that crack the code don't just capture most of the market—they disrupt entire industries, leaving competitors scrambling. If you're not prepared to evolve, you risk being disrupted.

This book will show you how to thrive in this new era. The future of your business depends on it.

What's Standing Between You and PLG Success?

While we've all heard of PLG success stories like Slack, Dropbox, and Canva, too many product-led companies fall far short.

After helping more than 400 companies implement PLG, these are the three most common pitfalls:

Pitfall 1: Approaching PLG as a "Product" Thing

This one is understandable. It's called "product-led growth," indicating that the product is a big piece of the puzzle. Where companies get themselves into trouble is thinking that PLG is solely a "product" initiative when, in reality, it needs to be a "company-wide" strategy.

A year ago, I was curious to know which of our clients were most successful, so I manually went through all 324 of them at the time. I analyzed the job titles of those we worked with, who brought their team along to learn, who rolled out a free motion, and who had a free motion that generated great results.

It was a lot of digging, but it was worth it.

At that time, our ideal customers—and 80% of our clients—were senior product executives. SaaS founders represented less than 20%.

Yet, when I analyzed who was most successful, I found that it was the SaaS founders. This blew my mind. The tiny 20% of SaaS founders were generating 80% of the results with their PLG motions.

Why weren't product executives as successful? What they often lacked was leadership buy-in. When we worked with SaaS founders, they implemented PLG as a company-wide initiative; it wasn't just for the product team.

When done right, PLG aligns how your entire company creates and captures value. Without organizational buy-in and a unified strategy, you risk treating PLG as just another product feature rather than a company-wide growth engine.

PLG is a go-to-market (GTM) motion, not a product strategy.

Pitfall 2: Not Providing Meaningful, Timely Value Before Monetizing

When you sign up for a free product, you make a snap decision on whether or not to move forward. If the product experience is clunky and frustrating, users won't come back. You do the same thing when you pilot products.

Some 40 to 60% of your first-time users sign up and never come back. You need to showcase value quickly. If you don't, customers will never upgrade without talking to you, if at all.

Pitfall 3: Not Executing Effectively

Most of us are terrible at new things. When I first learned to ski, I wiped out so often that I almost gave up—I wasn't having fun. As we get older, we expect to magically be great at new things and, more often than not, avoid them entirely and stick to what we already know. But the truth is, growth occurs when we make mistakes.

The same is true for PLG. An awkward learning phase is made worse by focusing on advanced steps like "nailing your product data" before you're even clear on your ideal user.

I recently chatted with a client about their low free-to-paid conversion rate. The founder confidently stated that he was going to invest the entire next quarter to improve his user onboarding with the Bowling Alley Framework. (I cover this in the Onboarding Component.) I was delighted to hear that he was putting the book into practice; however, I had a realization when I went to his site. I had zero clue what his company did. It was something AI-enabled if that gives you a hint.

I quickly pointed out that if users couldn't understand what his product did and the main value proposition, optimizing the onboarding would only offer a marginal improvement on his free-to-paid conversion rate, at best. But he could see a 10x impact by simplifying his offer on the homepage.

It was a deer-in-headlights realization for him.

These stories are all too common. We're so close to our business that it's easy to drink the jargon Kool-Aid and forget that what seems simple to us is puzzling to others.

It's normal to do stuff in the wrong order. There's no playbook for building and scaling a product-led business and no guarantee that the best product will win.

Far too often, sales-led companies capture more market share with an inferior product and user experience. The product-led founder, meanwhile, has invested far more to build a powerful product but can't get much traction because of a rickety GTM motion.

Whenever I see a product-led business lose to a sales-led company, it motivates me even more. Product-led businesses should win every time.

You've invested more time and energy. You care about delivering a fantastic experience. You believe serving users matters more than selling. You have a mission—to make your product better, faster, and cheaper.

As Jeff Bezos says, "The best entrepreneurs are missionaries instead of mercenaries. The mercenaries are just trying to make money, and paradoxically, the missionaries always end up making more money."

Product-led founders create enormous leverage through their products, build lean companies, and are highly profitable. This book will show you how to become a successful product-led founder and change the way you sell, forever.

To do that, you need to avoid one big trap.

"It's a Trap!"

Star Wars nerds know what I mean.

You arrive with your entourage of allies only to find out you're outgunned 10 to one, with no escape. You need to fight it out. Arghh!

Say you start rolling out PLG. You…

- Focus on launching a free trial or freemium model.
- Build out transparent pricing.
- Improve onboarding to get users to value more quickly.
- Update your homepage to get more free signups.

While these are all important aspects of PLG, they're only half the story.

This fundamental oversight is precisely why many fail to make PLG work.

I call this "surface-level PLG."

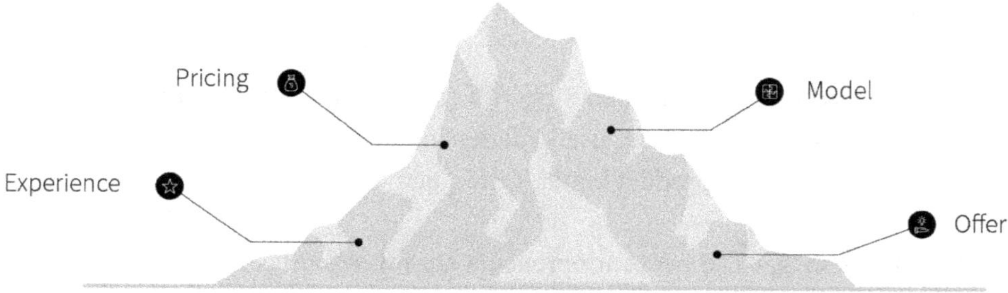

This leads to treating PLG as "a product thing," with:

1. No organizational buy-in.
2. Lackluster results.
3. Unfocused execution.
4. Not enough value before monetizing.

Businesses doing surface-level PLG often kill the motion entirely because it doesn't work.

This is what happened to us at Vidyard back in 2016.

We were trying to grow fast but had only a sales-led motion. Some of our competitors had a free trial, so we thought it was a good idea to try one ourselves. We created a landing page, funneled visitors to it, and gave them access to the product.

At first, the results were promising. We saw a surge of signups and thought we were on the right track. Three weeks later, not a single user upgraded without talking to sales. We even wondered if something was wrong with our product.

By the time we saw the problem, it was too late. We hit the hidden part of the iceberg at full speed. The free trial bombed. So we killed it.

What we lacked at Vidyard was everything below the surface that supports PLG.

PLG needs the right environment to thrive.

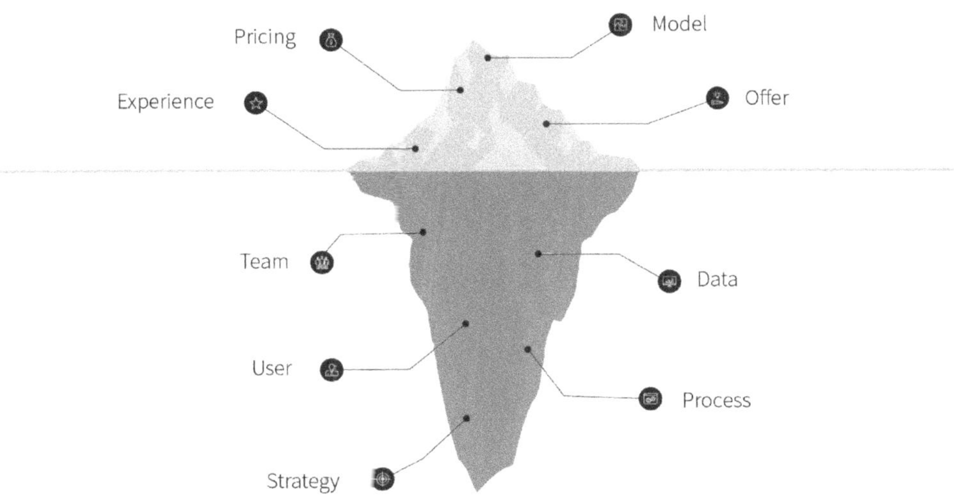

When trying to salvage our free trial experience at Vidyard, I approached key leaders with our plan of attack. Their answers were simply that the company had other priorities. It wasn't on the roadmap.

It's frustrating when there isn't alignment around how to approach PLG.

It can't thrive without:

- A company-level strategy in which PLG is a key part of winning in the market.

- Clarity on your ideal user. Most sales-led businesses know their ideal buyers well, but the *ideal* user—who is that?
- The faintest idea of what those users are doing in your product.
- The weekly rhythms in the business to identify what's bottlenecking users.
- An effective growth process to launch regular experiments to improve your experience.
- An elite team with the right capabilities to take PLG to the next level.

All that below-the-surface support is your product-led organization (PLO).

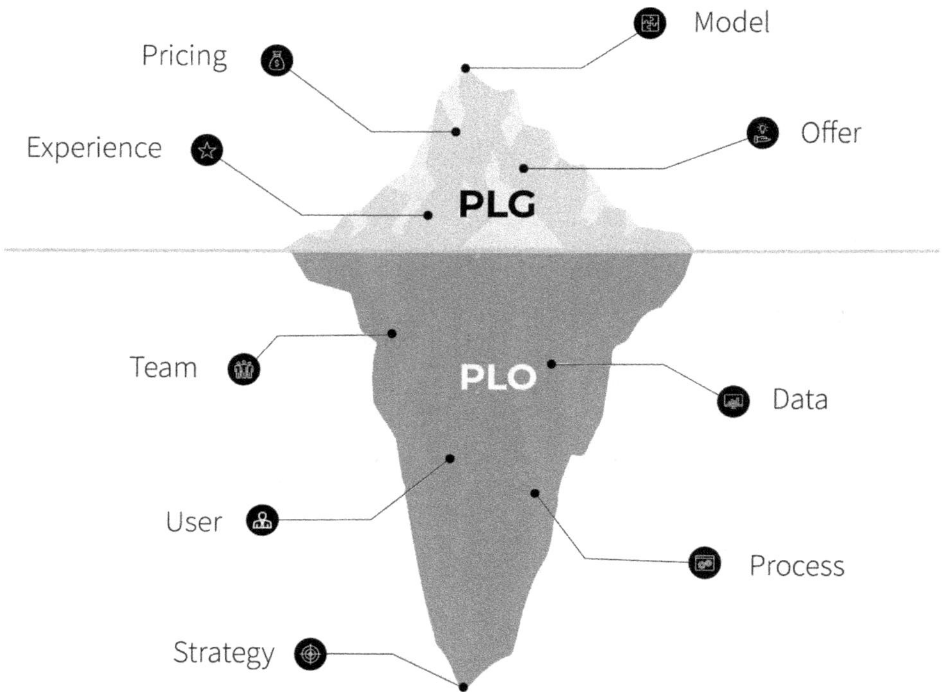

PLOs are the company-focused backbone that makes PLG happen. Simply put, PLG is everything the user interacts with on the front end, while your PLO ensures your company is aligned and firing on all cylinders on the back end.

Many companies try to deploy PLG without building a PLO. They launch a free trial, hoping it transforms how they sell, and then they notice it's not working. The reason is because they don't have a strong PLO to back it up.

Just like what happened at Vidyard.

To fully embrace PLG, you must transform *how* you sell and *how* you run your organization.

Instead of focusing solely on optimizing your PLG motion, ask: How can I design an organization so that PLG succeeds?

Becoming product-led is the integration of the two.

This book will help you become product-led.

When you do that, you can expect three outcomes.

1. **Effortless Annual Recurring Revenue (ARR):** Your product sells itself. Users can sign up, get value, and upgrade without talking to anyone.
2. **Lean Scale:** You generate substantial revenue with a tiny team. Your revenue per employee remains high because the product does the heavy lifting.
3. **Durable Growth:** You unlock more profits every year. Your lifetime customer value increases as users return to your product and use it more frequently.

If achieving these outcomes was easy, I wouldn't have written this book. And you wouldn't be reading it.

But you're here because you're ready to become product-led. In the next chapter, you'll discover the system that will empower you to do just that.

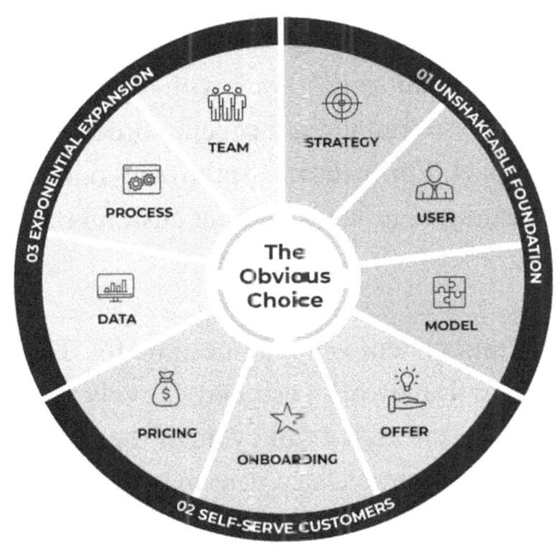

Introducing The ProductLed System™

The ProductLed System is your roadmap to scaling your product-led business and becoming the obvious choice in your market.

This isn't another theoretical framework—it's a system grounded in real-world experience, practical methods, and first-principles thinking. More importantly, it works. Over the years, through hands-on work with clients, I've developed a practical approach to help you build a world-class product-led business.

The ProductLed System focuses on nine key components for scaling a product-led business. These components embody the 80/20 Pareto principle: 80% of your results will come from just 20% of your efforts. By mastering these components, you'll realize your vision faster without working harder.

While the system is straightforward to understand, it requires time and effort to implement effectively within your organization. It didn't appear overnight; it's the culmination of over 10,000 hours of planning, teaching, coaching, and solving leadership challenges.

This system delivers three core outcomes: Effortless ARR, Lean Scale, and Durable Growth.

It's structured around three crucial stages, each with three distinct components. These components build on one another in a specific order, ensuring that your efforts yield maximum impact. For instance, optimizing onboarding without a clear offer is futile, and scaling your team without customer traction is a drain on resources.

It's important to note that this system is not a one-time fix. The ProductLed System is a living, breathing framework designed to evolve with your business. At a minimum, you should go through a full cycle of the system once a year. For fast-growing companies, up to four cycles a year may be necessary.

And it all starts with mastering the fundamentals.

Stage 1: Build an Unshakeable Foundation

You can't build a skyscraper on a shaky foundation.

During this stage, your job is to fine-tune the fundamentals of your product-led business so it can withstand the strain of significant growth. You'll craft a winning strategy to stand out from the competition, get to know your ideal users better than anyone in your market, and identify and refine the best product-led model.

You build the foundation by dialing in three critical components.

Winning Strategy

You must be crystal clear on what you do best and align that with market needs. You need a strategy to direct everyone's energy in one direction. Focus is key.

The Bullseye Strategy Framework will help you:

- Understand how to become the obvious choice in your market.

- Be crystal clear on what your company is really good at doing.
- Get a clear picture of what winning looks like for your business.
- Design a business that is hard to copy.

The next step is to define your ideal user.

Ideal User

The truth is, most companies think they understand their users deeply, but they don't. The ones that do, however, capture the maximum market share by knowing their users better than anyone else.

Users are the lifeblood of any product-led business. You need to know your users well. In this component, you'll go through how to understand your users better than anyone else in your market. You'll go beyond just understanding their job-to-be-done and put yourself in their shoes to understand what they think, feel, and do at each stage of interacting with your product.

After installing the User Endgame Roadmap, your entire organization will:

- Know your best users.
- Align on the endgame for your users.
- Know users' top challenges.

When you know what makes your users tick, you can proactively address challenges and design a product-led model that helps users accomplish something meaningful, albeit for free.

Intentional Model

A product-led model determines what you give away for free and what you gate behind a paywall. A good product-led model gives users everything they need to see incredible value. A bad product-led model typically fails to deliver enough value. The telltale sign of a bad product-led model is a low free-to-paid conversion rate.

I'll help you identify the right product-led model for your ideal users—one where they can experience the right value and feel tempted to upgrade.

With the DEEP Model Framework, you'll:

- Gamify your user journey.
- Decide what to give away for free vs. what to monetize.
- Identify what model works best for your business (i.e. freemium, free trial, etc.).

Once you've built an unshakeable foundation, you're ready for users to upgrade without talking to you.

Stage 2: Unlock Self-Serve Customers

The second stage builds a product that sells itself. The monumental shift is changing *how* you sell. By providing incredible value before monetizing users, you make upgrading a no-brainer.

The goal is to move from high-touch to zero-touch. But that can only happen if users can sign up, get to value, and upgrade without talking to you. That's how you achieve Lean Scale and Effortless ARR.

To do that, you must craft an irresistible offer.

Irresistible Offer

Crafting an irresistible offers requires understanding three undeniable facts about your product:

1. What are the results of using your product?
2. Why is there less risk when using your product?
3. How is your product better than the competition or alternative solutions?

The tricky part is communicating this quickly so that users immediately understand what you do, especially if you're not in a well-established category.

The 5-Star Offer Generator ensures you have:

- A compelling core offer.
- More ideal users signing up for your offer.
- A higher free-to-paid conversion rate.

Once you've got more motivated users than you can handle, it's time to improve onboarding.

Frictionless Onboarding

Leverage comes from making it easy for users to sign up, get to value, and upgrade. Eliminating friction is how you do it.

The Bowling Alley Framework will show you how to:

- Create a fast path for users to experience value.
- Add bumpers to make it effortless to get to value.
- Proactively support users when they drop off.

By the end of the Onboarding Component, the percentage of users who experience the full value of your product will skyrocket.

Then, it's time for them to upgrade.

Powerful Pricing

To turn users into high-paying customers without talking to you, you must offer transparent, strategic pricing that is simple to understand. A strategic pricing model starts at an accessible level and scales as the user derives more value from the product. Costs grow in line with the value the user achieves.

With the Value Ladder Framework, you'll:

- Have more free users upgrading to a paid plan.
- Unlock higher customer lifetime value.
- Increase net revenue retention (NRR).

Altogether, these three components unlock self-serve customers. At this point, you're ready for exponential expansion.

Stage 3: Ignite Exponential Expansion

Finally, the third phase is all about structuring your team and processes to 10x their impact, transitioning you from incremental to exponential growth. Actionable data is the starting point.

Actionable Data

Most companies have complex scorecards and track too many metrics. You need simplicity to understand your business' core bottleneck.

With the True North Framework, you'll:

- Identify the North Star metric to align your entire company.
- Provide a simple scorecard to break down your GTM and financial metrics.
- Pinpoint your #1 bottleneck so you always know where to focus.

Once you know the bottleneck, you must have the growth process in place to eliminate it.

Growth Process

To attain predictable growth, your entire team must translate action into results.

When you install the Predictable Growth Process, you'll:

- Establish consistent rhythms to evaluate the company's performance and proactively launch experiments to tackle your biggest bottleneck.
- Turn your entire company into a growth team.
- Accelerate execution.

With this process, you'll gain momentum as a team and grow faster as a byproduct. The final component is all about building an elite team.

Elite Team

In a product-led business, your product is the machine, not your team. That's what gives you leverage and helps you maintain lean scale with a high revenue per employee (RPE).

With the Elite Team Flywheel, you'll:

- Increase your RPE by designing a lean team.

- Uplevel the performance of your team.
- Align incentives so everyone rows in the same direction.

Altogether, the Data, Process, and Team Components ignite exponential expansion and profitability through focus. You zero in on high-confidence bets and go all-in with your resources.

Install Your Operating System

The ProductLed System is a GTM Operating System for your business.

Just like your computer runs Windows or macOS, your company has an operating system, too. To stay relevant and protect yourself from threats, you need to update each component throughout the year or, at the very least, review them to ensure they're still relevant.

When you consistently update the ProductLed System, you'll stay ahead of market trends, address opportunities sooner, and grow faster. That's why at ProductLed, we continually refine the ProductLed System, using insights from hundreds of clients to adapt to new market conditions and optimize what works.

One of the most common pieces of feedback I get from founders who implement the ProductLed System for the first time is that they end up working less but have way more impact.

That's my goal for you—to move from frenetic to focused, with a sustainable pace of execution that provides more bang for your buck. How close are you to that right now?

Define Your Starting Point

Understanding where your company stands is crucial to making the ProductLed System work for you. By pinpointing your current position, you can track the tangible impact the system has on your business. This will help you see the cause and effect as you move closer to becoming the obvious choice in your market.

Benchmark your business in three core areas.

Effortless ARR

How can you build a product that sells itself?

The main metric is self-serve revenue (SSR). SSR is truly effortless ARR because users can sign up, get to value, and upgrade without talking to you.

Benchmark where you are today by placing an X in the column that best describes the current level of your business:

	Level 1	Level 2	Level 3	Level 4
SSR Ranges	**\$0 to \$1M** *Tiresome Customers*	**\$1M to \$5M** *Sporadic Sales*	**\$5M to \$20M** *Predictable Revenue*	**\$20M to \$50M+** *Absolute Leverage*
Current Level				
Next Level				

Take a minute to reflect on where you want to be in the next three years. Choose at least one level up from where you are today.

If you're already at Level 4, write down what Level 5 will be for you (e.g., \$100M or \$200M+ SSR).

After analyzing thousands of businesses, only 5% achieved more than \$10M SSR.[4] The rest have, at best, sporadic sales.

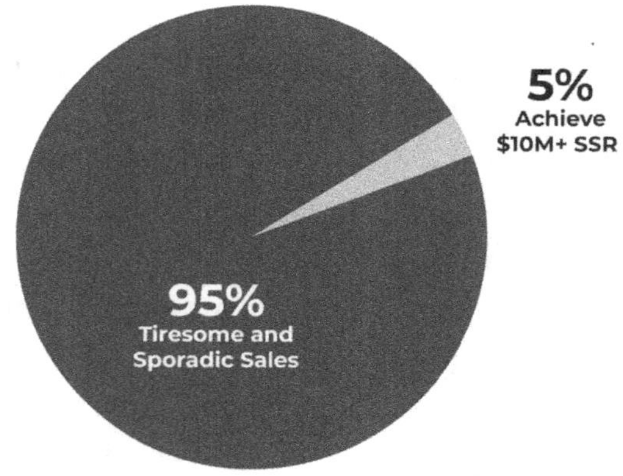

**As of August 27, 2024*
**Source: ProductLed Index, based on data collected from 2043 SaaS businesses from 2023-2024.*

The ProductLed System will help you skyrocket your SSR and get you into the top 5%.

Lean Scale

How can you build a big business with a tiny team?

A tenet of building a product-led business is that your product does more heavy lifting as you scale.

The main metric is your revenue per employee (RPE). Calculate this by dividing your total revenue by the number of employees you have. For example, if your revenue is $1M this year and you have 10 full-time employees, your RPE is $100,000.

$$\frac{\textbf{1,000,000}}{\textbf{10 Employees}} = \textbf{\$100,000 RPE}$$

A high RPE means you're efficient and have a product that does the heavy lifting. A low RPE typically means your business is overly reliant on people.

Benchmark where you are today and where you want to be in three years:

	Level 1	Level 2	Level 3	Level 4
RPE Ranges	**$0 to $100k** *Treading Water*	**$100k to $300k** *Streamlined Company*	**$300k to $700k** *Prolific Performers*	**$1M to $2M+** *Ace Team*
Current Level				
Next Level				

If you're already at Level 4, write down what Level 5 will be for you (i.e., $3 to $5M RPE). Only 4% of companies ever enjoy an RPE of $1M+.[5]

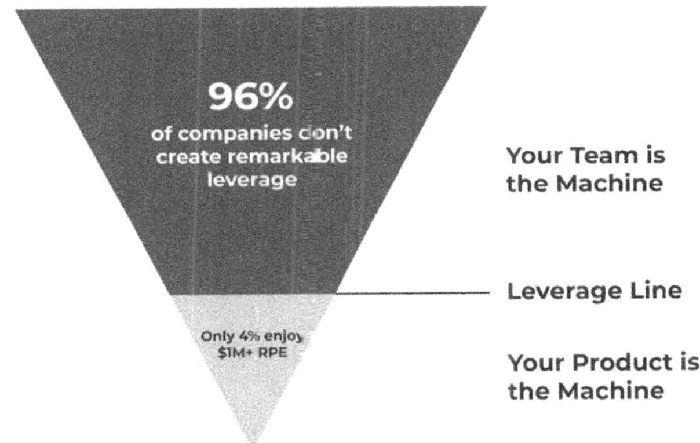

**As of August 27, 2024*
**Source: ProductLed Index, based on data collected from 2043 SaaS businesses from 2023-2024.*

Everything above the "Leverage Line" means that your team, not the product, is the machine.

Companies without leverage often find themselves trapped in a cycle of overwork and inefficiency. Instead of effortless scale, growth demands more resources and manual effort. This not only limits profitability but also stifles innovation. Operational demands consume the team and reduce bandwidth for forward-thinking initiatives.

To break from this cycle, shift your focus from scaling through people to scaling through products. **Your product should be your best employee, salesperson, and customer service rep.**

It drives revenue, attracts customers, and scales effortlessly—all while your lean team focuses on steering the boat, not rowing it. Companies that achieve this level of efficiency and leverage dominate their markets.

Sustaining that dominance requires durable growth.

Durable Growth

How can you unlock more profits every year?

A lack of profitability makes companies fragile. One little bump in the road can be fatal.

A company with high profitability can withstand many bumps but isn't invincible. For instance, a CEO could simply harvest profits for short-term gains at the expense of marketing and product development.

You want durable growth—profits that increase every year like clockwork. This requires your business to evolve to cope with ever-changing market demands.

Mark your net profit for today and where you want to be:

	Level 1	Level 2	Level 3	Level 4
Profit Ranges	**$0 to $100k** *Tiny Profits*	**$100k to $1M** *Small Reserve*	**$1M to $5M** *Fair Fortune*	**$5M to $10M** *Automatic Profits*
Current Level				
Next Level				

You might be thinking that this metric doesn't really measure year-over-year profit growth. You're right.

Most companies we work with start with small profits. We need to help them get to sizable profits before we start worrying about annual profit growth. Tracking these profit milestones is good enough for 95% of founders.

If you've already hit "Automatic Profits," congrats! You can swap out measuring profit for Net Profit Growth Rate. Here's the formula:

$$\textbf{Net Profit Growth Rate} = \frac{\textbf{Net Profit This Year - Net Profit Last Year}}{\textbf{Net Profit Last Year}}$$

For example, if your company's net profit was $500,000 last year and increased to $600,000 this year, the Net Profit Growth Rate would be 20%.

$$\frac{600{,}000 - 500{,}000}{500{,}000} \times 100 = 20\%$$

Where do you stack up today, and where do you want to be?

Net Profit Growth Rate Ranges	**Level 1** **0 to 10%** *Inflationary Growth*	**Level 2** **11 to 20%** *Solid Growth*	**Level 3** **21 to 49%** *Breakout Growth*	**Level 4** **50%+** *Hypergrowth*
Current Level				
Next Level				

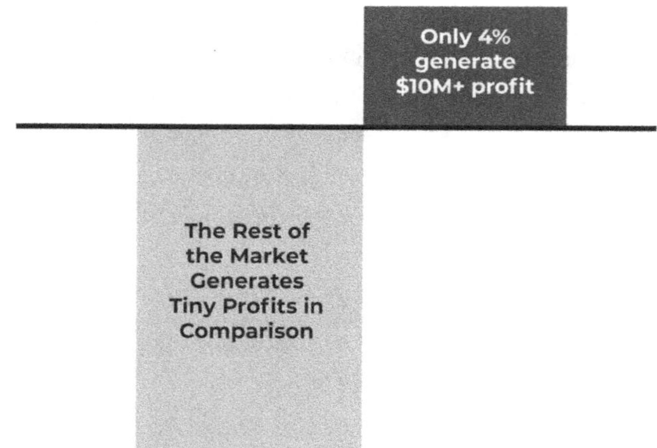

**As of August 27, 2024*
**Source: ProductLed Index, based on data collected from 2043 SaaS businesses from 2023-2024.*

Only 4% of companies ever generate $10M+ profits.[6] Why? Because the market leader becomes the obvious choice and enjoys **automatic profits**.

When you become the obvious choice, users and customers all refer your product to their friends and colleagues. That's the goal.

As a product-led founder, you've invested more time and energy in building your product than anyone else. You have a mission to make whatever you do more accessible, affordable, or simple.

Your product deserves to become the obvious choice in your market. Let's get to work.

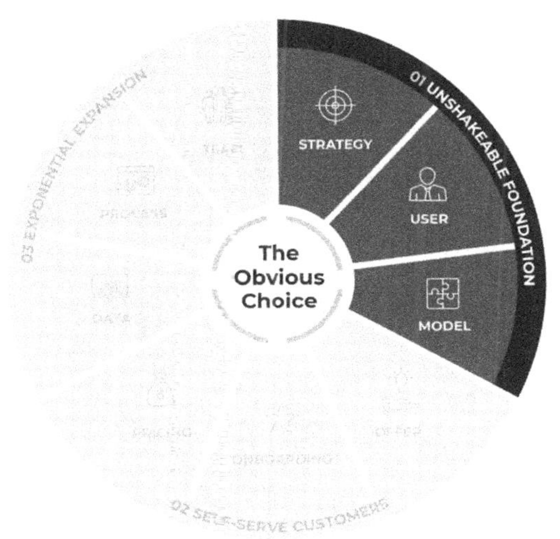

Stage 1

Build an Unshakeable Foundation

Go from “scattered” to “streamlined.”

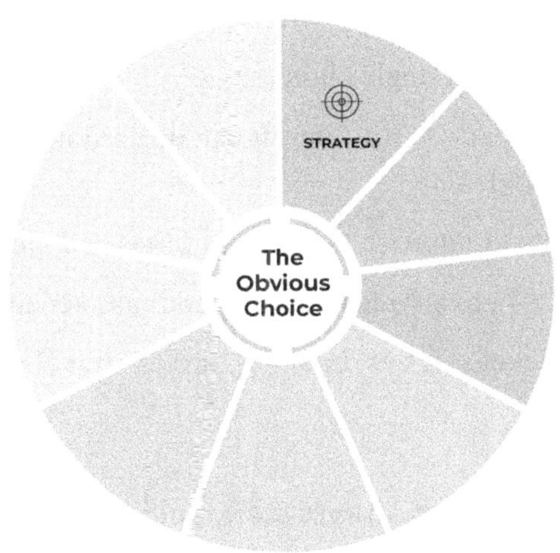

Winning Strategy

How clearly are you the **obvious choice** for customers in your market?

Barely Noticeable | Fairly Apparent | Universally Recognized

Rate yourself from 1 to 10.

A strategy is not a plan; it's a theory on how you will win.

For instance, Southwest Airlines wanted to be the obvious choice for travelers seeking an alternative to Greyhound.

They believed they could win a substantial part of the market by offering low-cost airline tickets while maintaining the lowest costs to run their business.

To do that, they made key strategic choices:

1. Fly point-to-point routes so the aircraft can be used more than the typical hub-and-spoke model.
2. No meals on flights to improve turnaround times and cleanup.
3. Fly only Boeing 737s to simplify training and maintenance costs.
4. Prioritize online ticket sales vs. booking through travel agents to increase their margin.

This strategy helped Southwest Airlines scale rapidly. By 2023, it flew the most passenger-seat miles in the United States.[7] They've fallen from grace on the public relations front, but that reinforces an important point.

At the core of a winning business strategy is the choice to do some things and not others. Southwest Airlines couldn't have won by following other airlines. It had to say no to long-distance flights, partnering with travel agents, and flying different aircraft.

A winning business strategy makes it easier for your team to say no to initiatives and projects that don't align with your theory of how you're going to win. It's not easy.

When a strong bias for action is present in a company, you can fall into the "action trap" of trying to do everything instead of being intentional about what you won't pursue. A good strategy helps the company know what is and isn't important. This creates a relentless focus that intentionally directs everyone's energy. A bad strategy, on the other hand, wastes countless resources and energy by trying to do it all.

In *Essentialism*, Greg McKeown points out that if you have 10 units of energy, you could broadcast it in 10 different directions to make one inch of progress in each direction. Or you could put all that energy into one direction and make 10 inches of progress.

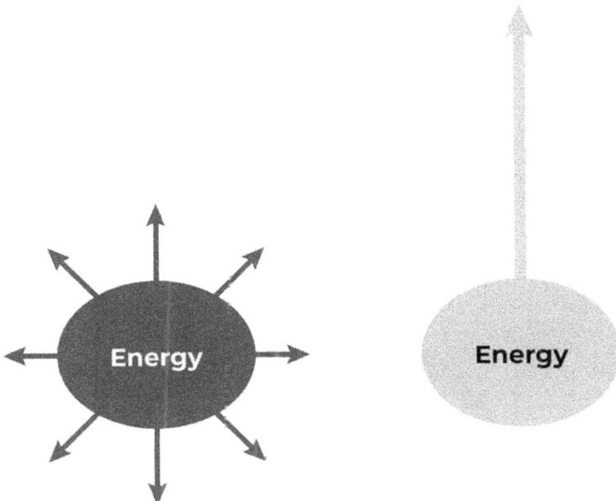

A great strategy unites your team to make massive progress in one direction by giving everyone the same decision-making framework for the company's focus.

Focus means:

- Your entire team can make decisions faster.
- Your customers better understand what you do.
- Your business becomes hard to copy.

I would know, but not for the reasons you might think.

For the first five years of running ProductLed, we had no winning strategy. Our target market was vague, and we didn't have a distinct advantage. My bias for action was running the day-to-day. We got a lot done, but few projects made a big impact. Over time, we lost momentum and were pushing a rock up a hill.

Then, we built a strategy with this framework. We became intentional about where we directed our energy. We said no to exciting opportunities to pursue ones aligned with our strengths.

Over time, growth picked up. We started making massive progress in *one* direction.

The Bullseye Strategy Framework

What sparked this transition for me was reading Roger Martin and A.G. Lafley's *Playing to Win*, which outlines their strategic framework for Fortune 500 companies.

I found it a tad clunky for SaaS businesses, so I simplified their approach to create the Bullseye Strategy Framework. It consists of five steps that underpin your high-level strategy.

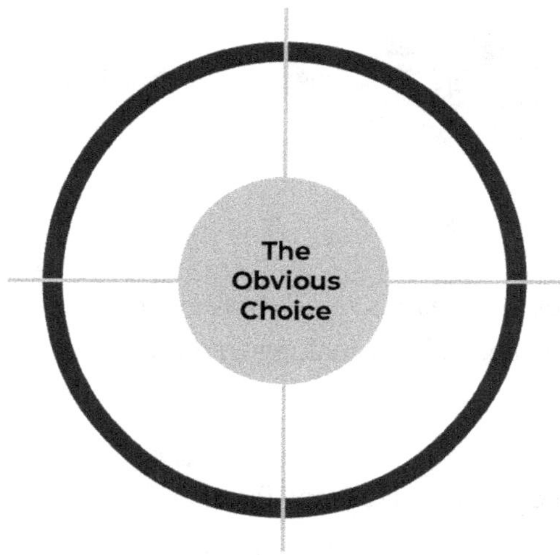

Step 1: Which Market Can You Dominate as the Obvious Choice?

Every market becomes commoditized.

In a commoditized market, it's a race to become the obvious choice.

There's only one Canva.

One HubSpot.
One Atlassian.
One Zoom.

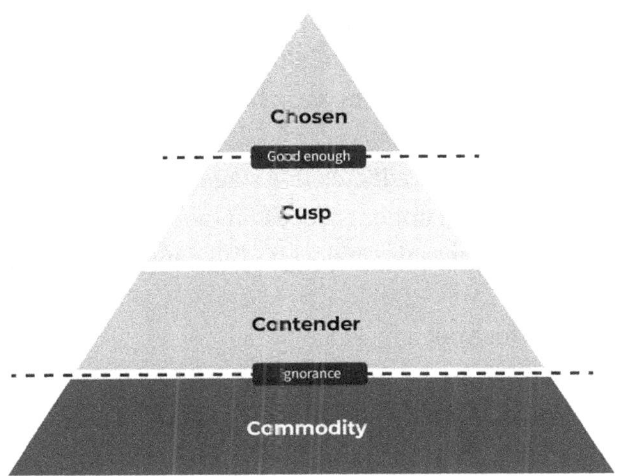

In the early stages, many businesses find themselves in what's known as the **Commodity** zone. The struggle is real here: competition is fierce, and profits are slim. At this point, your product doesn't stand out, so it becomes difficult to command higher prices or attract customers easily. The customers you do manage to acquire often need a lot of hands-on help to use your product effectively. This stage demands significant effort just to convince users to sign up for your product, not to mention getting them to realize its value.

This is where so many teams get stuck.

There is too much at stake to be simply a commodity.

To reach the next level, your product needs to start doing the heavy lifting to support users so you can get out of day-to-day operations.

That's when you become an actual **Contender** in your market. It's not a bad place to be, but to get to the next level, you need a killer strategy that makes you differentiate and stand out from the rest of the competition.

That's when you're on the **Cusp** in your specific industry. You're one of the top three to five players in your space. When you're at this stage, it's actually great. Usually, you have seven-figure profits, a high RPE, and predictable revenue in your business.

But it's not the final stage. In fact, this is the most dangerous place. This is where most stop. Good enough is the enemy of a truly great business. This is where it really takes discipline. And that is why very few make it to the top.

At the top, you're the **Chosen** leader. At this stage, you're the Canva of your industry. Your strategy should not only focus on outshining competitors but also on scaling efficiently to capture the majority of the market share.

Now I have a question for you...

Which market can you dominate as the obvious choice?

Many founders often feel intimidated and question their ability to become the obvious choice. To overcome this reluctance, specify who you're targeting and your unique value. For example, if you're a CRM tool competing against HubSpot, it's unlikely you'll beat them by also targeting all small-to-medium-sized businesses (SMBs). To win, you must target a segment of the market. Instead, you could focus on being the best CRM for real estate agents.

One of our ProductLed clients, Paubox, offers HIPAA compliance for health professionals. Could they win the market for *all* health professionals? Maybe. But the better play for now is becoming the best solution for one segment: mental health professionals.

Obvious Choice Statement
We are the obvious choice for mental health professionals who struggle with HIPAA email compliance.

As you think through who and what you're the obvious choice for, permit yourself to dream. Think big. The whole point is to set a direction for your business. If it feels audacious, that might be a sign you're pushing the bounds too far. You want to feel like you can dominate this market confidently. Remember: you're going to update this strategy consistently throughout the year, so start small and slowly expand your vision.

Your Turn (To Fill In)

Obvious Choice Statement

Once you're clear on that, dig into where to play.

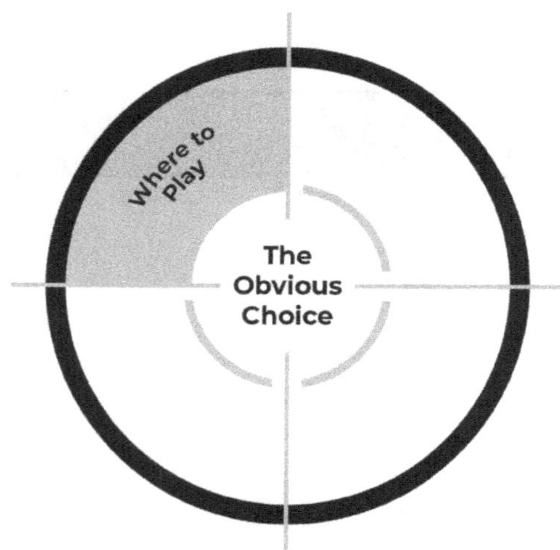

Step 2: Where Will You Play?

Where you play is as much art as science.

I wish I could say it's as simple as picking a target market and a marketing channel. But no matter how you approach it, there's an awkward trial-and-error phase until you find where you play best.

Start by answering five questions:

1. Who's your ideal customer? Define the group that loves your product for what it is today.
2. What problem do you solve? Identify the meaningful problem your business addresses.
3. What's your core product? Focus on the product that drives most of your revenue.
4. What are your primary marketing channels? Choose the main channels that generate traffic and signups.
5. What geography do you target? Concentrate on regions with the most ideal customers.

Be specific. Avoid the temptation to be everything to everybody. Paubox realized they could win the market by focusing solely on email compliance.

Ideal Customer	Mental health professional at a single location
Main Problem	HIPAA email compliance
Core Product	Email suite
Primary Marketing Channels	Organic Search
Geography	United States

When you're not intentional about where you play, you spread yourself too thin. An army trying to fight multiple battles always gets destroyed by an army focused on a single beachhead.

To clarify which marketing channels to pursue, read *Traction: How Any Startup Can Achieve Explosive Growth* by Gabriel Weinberg and Justin Mares. This book is one of the best at outlining what marketing channels make the most sense for your business.

Your Turn (To Fill In)

Ideal Customer	
Main Problem	
Core Product	
Primary Marketing Channels	
Geography	

Once you know where to play, it's time to create a game plan for winning.

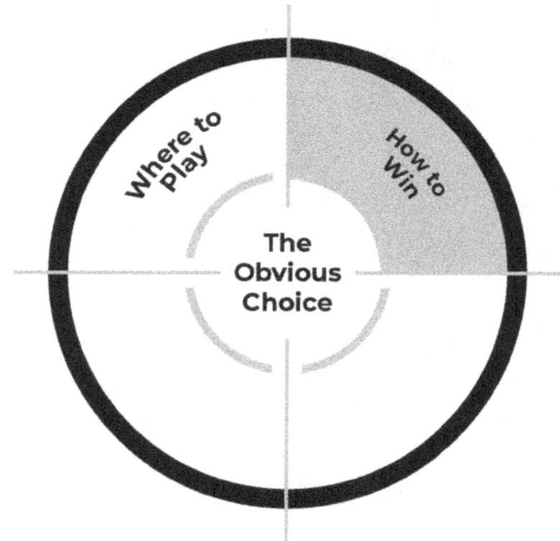

Step 3: How Will You Win?

Starting a business has never been easier, so competition is fierce. Copying your product isn't hard.

So, what makes your business hard to copy? Moats.

When I lived in Chiang Mai, Thailand, they had an ancient moat that surrounded the entire city in a square. This gave defenders two huge advantages:

1. Offenders had to swim across the water.
2. Then they had to climb the walls.

Whoever tried to invade the city was at a serious disadvantage.

A moat works the same way in business. It gives your company true defensibility and makes you hard to copy.

You can and should build more than one moat over time. Ideally, you have three. A competitor might be able to copy one moat, but copying all three is nearly impossible.

There are countless potential moats, but these are 15 of the best:

Differentiation Moat: Offer a unique product or service that fulfills customer needs in a distinct and valuable way. This could involve innovative features, superior quality, focusing on a specific niche, or a combination of factors.

Cost Leadership Moat: Become the low-cost provider in your industry while maintaining acceptable quality standards. Achieve cost advantages through economies of scale and efficient operations.

User Experience Moat: Create a seamless and intuitive user experience (UX) and extend that same level of thought and care throughout the customer journey. Understand customers' needs and preferences to design seamless, personalized interactions and build long-term loyalty.

Network Effects Moat: Network effects occur when the value of a product or service increases as more people use it. Examples include social media platforms like Meta, where more users make the platform more valuable for each user. You can see network effects at companies like Webflow, WordPress, Miro, and Canva, where armies of users create templates for others.

Operational Efficiency Moat: Streamline your internal processes and optimize resource allocation to improve productivity and reduce costs. Efficient operations lead to better profitability, faster delivery times, and improved customer satisfaction.

Branding and Reputation Moat: Build a strong brand that resonates with your target audience. Cultivate a positive reputation by consistently delivering on your promises, providing exceptional products or services, and actively engaging with your customers. A notable brand can command customer loyalty, trust, and premium pricing.

Distribution Moat: An extensive distribution network or exclusive access to key channels, strategic partnerships, and alliances creates barriers for competitors. It allows businesses to reach customers more effectively and control the availability of their products or services.

For example, when your app is one of the first in the Shopify or Android app stores, you get the lion's share of the downloads, and, over time, your app gains the most reviews and attention, which is hard to replicate.

We benefited from this in the early days of PLG. We wrote a lot of great content on the subject before people were talking about it. Over time, we gained a ton of backlinks and authority around the topic, generating traffic that's hard for new entrants to copy.

Speed and Innovation Moat: Rapid innovation is one of the most underrated moats. *It's not the big that eats the small... It's the fast that eats the slow.* It's also a great book written by Jason Jennings and Laurence Haughton on how to use speed as a competitive advantage. You can stand out if you break into a stagnant industry.

Pricing Moat: A unique pricing strategy that aligns with customer success can give you a strong competitive edge. For example, you could offer your product for free and cover costs through sponsorships, charge only when users get value by taking a percentage of each transaction, or, like Basecamp and Flodesk, avoid charging for additional users, unlike most companies.

Free Moat: Just having a free product experience for users is a start, but you can take this even further by creating more free products subsidized by your core product(s). Expand into adjacent markets and disrupt them by promoting your product for free to capture more potential users and demand for your other products. For example, ConvertKit, an email marketing tool, created a free landing page tool to make it easier for creators to capture signups.

Switching Cost Moat: A business can create high switching costs for customers through contractual obligations, integration with other systems, or data lock-in. Designing your software to create switching costs for customers can reduce churn. For instance, Alina Vandenberghe, co-CEO at Chili Piper, reduced churn by 35% for organizations with three or more integrations by integrating their platform with other tools.

Proprietary Moat: Patents, trademarks, copyrights, and trade secrets protect a company's intellectual property and provide a competitive advantage by preventing others from replicating or using proprietary technologies or brands. For instance, we developed the ProductLed System™ as our proprietary process to help software founders scale their self-serve revenue faster.

Engagement Moat: A vibrant brand community and active user engagement creates a loyal customer base and word-of-mouth marketing. Businesses that create a sense of belonging, encourage user-generated content and facilitate community interaction develop strong moats.

Expansion Moat: The main way to ensure you can spend the most to acquire a customer is by making the most per customer in your industry. This could be because each customer eventually buys more than one product from you, or you have a revenue model and high customer loyalty that grows customers' lifetime value over time.

HubSpot is a great example of winning with expansion. You start with their free CRM and sales tools when you're getting your first few customers. Then, when you have a good number of contacts, you start paying for their Marketing hub, and when you have a sales team, you can upgrade to their Sales hub. When you have too many customers to deal with, you can upgrade to their Service hub. One $50/month customer can eventually turn into a $5,000/month one.

Founder Brand Moat: Whether you decide to build in public or share content consistently on social, building a founder brand moat is hard to copy. Do you want to do business with a company where you feel like you know the founder or go with a faceless competitor? Adam Robinson from RB2B.com, Dave Gerhardt from Exit Five, Guillaume Moubeche from Lemlist, Jason Fried from 37signals, and Olly Meakings from Senja do an incredible job here.

Let me share four common scenarios of how you can build moats:

Be the low-cost leader in your market: Southwest Airlines decided to win through Cost Leadership and Operational Efficiency. These two moats complement each other: Lower costs bring in more customers, while operational efficiency preserves profitability.

Go upmarket: Consider making Differentiation, Customer Experience, and High Switching Costs your strengths. With these three, you'll better serve enterprise customers with your unique, differentiated solution and keep them with exceptional customer experience and high switching costs.

Become the dominant market leader: Consider building moats around Cost Leadership, Operational Efficiency, and User Experience. A great user experience drives operational efficiency (i.e., fewer support tickets and demos) and enables you to sell your product at a lower price with healthy margins. To keep the dominant market leadership position, your product must be better, faster, and cheaper than alternatives. These three moats do just that.

Disrupt a stagnant industry: Consider winning with a Free moat, Speed, and Cost Leadership. You can create a vacuum for unsatisfied customers typically over-served by the current enterprise solutions. (Hello, Canva versus Photoshop.) When you enter a stagnant industry with speed, incumbents can't keep up.

One of the fun parts about developing moats is that each can and should complement the others. It should feel like you're building a winning recipe. Individually, they're not that special. But together, they create an unstoppable combination that packs a real punch.

Here's an example from Paubox:

Moats	Reason
Differentiation Moat	Method of sending encrypted emails has patented IP.
User and Customer Experience Moat	Ideal users value an easy-to-use solution. They want to use their existing email solution but be HIPAA compliant.
Customer Support Moat	Ideal users aren't technical and need help integrating their solution with Google Workspace or Microsoft Outlook.

It's important to note that you can and should build more than one of these moats over time. Each creates a barrier to entry, making it harder for competitors to copy what you do.

And most importantly…

Creates a competitive advantage for you to win as a business.

Yet, you don't want to focus on building too many moats simultaneously. I recommend starting with one or two moats at a time, and once you've built them up, consider adding another.

Your Turn (To Fill In)

Moats	Reason

One important thing to point out here is that a moat is something you regularly need to maintain. It's not something you set and forget. For instance, if you have a Differentiation Moat with a couple of unique features but a competitor copies them, it's only a matter of time before your Differentiation Moat evaporates as customers see fewer differences between your offering and the competition.

As you map out which moats will help your business win, remember this is a theory on how you're going to win. The goal is to gain confidence about how you will win and ensure that you have the right capabilities to do so.

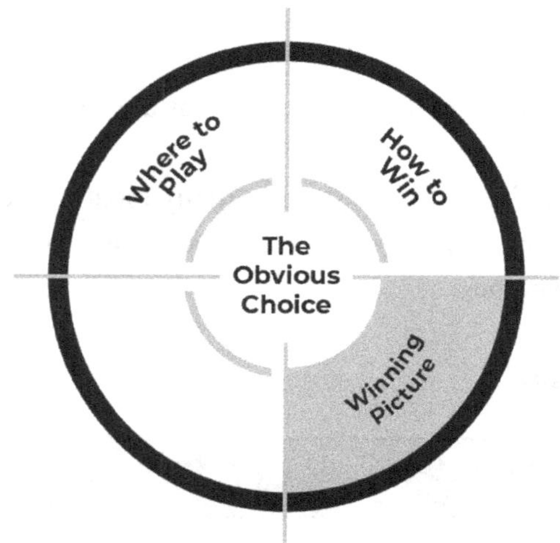

Step 4: What Is Your Winning Picture?

If your team has a different definition of winning, what are the odds you're going to win?

Slim to none.

Let's take a page from sports teams at the elite level.

The National Football League (NFL) has the Superbowl. Cyclists have the Tour de France. Tennis has Wimbledon.

If you're a professional athlete, winning at those events is the endgame.

If you're playing to win, you must have an endgame.

Yet, in business, that endgame is often vague for your team.

The most common endgames are:

1. Exiting the business
2. Initial Public Offering (IPO)
3. Profitability and financial success
4. Social impact and corporate responsibility
5. Customer impact

If your endgame is "to leave a legacy," that's not super specific. Your endgame needs to be SMART, as in Specific, Measurable, Achievable, Relevant, and Time-Bound.

That way, the rest of your team can understand the objective and know whether you're getting closer to achieving it.

Here are a few more specific examples

1. To reach $100M in revenue by the end of 2040.
2. To exit the business for $60M in the next five years.
3. To serve 10,000 customers in the next five years.
4. To transition the company to 100% employee ownership by 2032.
5. To build a community of one million engaged users by 2030.

For your timeline, pick something further out than three years but less than 10 years.

Your Turn (To Fill In)

Endgame

Now that you know your endgame, paint a picture of what winning looks like.

1-Year Picture

In one year, what does success look like for your business? How much revenue? Profit? What does the team look like? RPE?

By investing time in building your 1-Year Picture, you'll align your team, encourage big thinking, and create focus.

Start with identifying where you want to be across the Top Outcomes: revenue, RPE, and profit.

Choose three Top Goals for the year. These are directional and should be SMART.

For example, a Top Goal for the year at ProductLed is to launch this book and sell 5,000 copies.

Keep it simple.

Here's an example:

1-Year Picture	
Date	Dec 31, 2025
Top Outcomes	1. Revenue: $10M 2. RPE: $333,000 3. Profit: $3M
Top Annual Goals	1. Sell 5,000 copies of book. 2. 1,000 customers. 3. Founder is replaced with CEO.
Reward	Company retreat 🏖️

A reward is optional but boosts motivation and gamifies goals. Something at stake creates an incentive for the team to go the extra mile. We'll dive deeper into this in the Team Component, but for now, add a placeholder and see if it increases your drive to achieve the winning picture.

A good 1-Year Picture will give you a high-level overview of what the business looks like without getting bogged down.

Your Turn (To Fill In)

1-Year Picture	
Date	
Top Outcomes	
Top Annual Goals	
Reward	

Once you have your 1-Year Picture, paint a picture of what your business will look like in the next quarter.

Quarterly Picture

The main difference between the 1-Year Picture and Quarterly Picture is that everything in the quarter should get you closer to supporting your 1-Year Picture.

Here's an example:

Quarterly Picture	
Date	March 31, 2025
Top Outcomes	1. Revenue: $3M 2. Profit: $1M
Top Quarterly Goals	1. Launch bestselling book. 2. 100 active customers that love our product. 3. Hire two ProductLed Implementers.
Reward	Spa day for everyone on the team.

Your Quarterly Goals should directly support your Annual Goals.

Your Turn (To Fill In)

Quarterly Picture	
Date	
Top Outcomes	
Top Quarterly Goals	
Reward	

Now that you're aligned on the Quarterly Picture, it's time to define what winning looks like this month.

Monthly Picture

There's a saying: "Great years come from great quarters. Great quarters come from great months. Great months come from great weeks, and great weeks come from great days." While we won't go that granular, aligning your team around what winning looks like each month is a powerful step. This increases your chances of hitting quarterly and annual goals.

The key difference between the Quarterly Picture and Monthly Picture is focus. Focus drives massive progress, and a focused team will always outperform an unfocused one.

Here's how it works: start by deciding on the Top Focus for the month. Keep it simple and stick to one. Then, identify the Top Monthly Projects that directly support achieving that focus.

Make sure all of your resources are aligned to these projects, and that the team fully supports them. Here's an example:

Monthly Picture	
Date	Sept 30, 2024
Top Outcomes	1. Revenue: $700,000 2. Profit: $300,000
Top Focus	Launch the Product-Led Playbook
Top Monthly Projects	1. Record the audiobook. 2. Finish the templates. 3. Publish the book on Amazon.
Reward	Friday Off

Your Turn (To Fill In)

Monthly Picture	
Date	
Top Outcomes	
Top Focus	
Top Monthly Projects	
Reward	

You'll update your winning picture every month in the Process Component, so you always know what success looks like and can stay focused on achieving it.

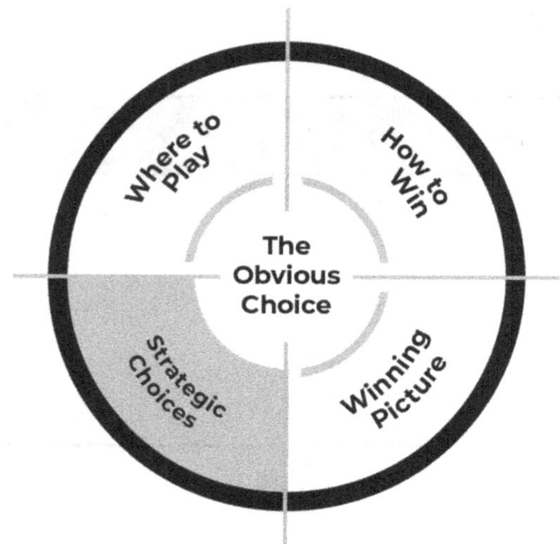

Step 5: What Strategic Choices Must You Make?

What you don't pursue is just as important as what you do pursue.

Some strategic choices are sacrifices. You won't make progress if you don't say no to good ideas, products, and even teammates.

The answers to two strategic questions will have an outsized impact on your business:

1. What are your core values?
2. What are the core capabilities your business needs?

Each has a cascading effect. Let's break down how to identify them.

Core Values

Your core values aren't just a slogan. You should hire and fire based on core values. Your core values should directly support your how-to-win strategy.

Currently, only 23% of employees believe in their organization's core values.[8] By aligning your values with your company strategy, you create a trustworthy foundation, reinforcing your unique approach to serving the market.

For instance, at ProductLed, we help our clients succeed with PLG. We couldn't do this effectively without our core value of simplicity. This value is central to who we are and helps us better serve clients.

What are the three qualities your company needs to serve your ideal customers better than others? Aim for three. Less is more. Most people forget a long list.

Your Turn (To Fill In)

Core Values

If you're stuck, ask yourself what bothers you about how some companies treat you. Your core values may simply be the opposite of what frustrates you.

With core values in place, you can identify the capabilities you need to succeed.

Capabilities

A capability directly supports your ability to win.

Say you want to be an Olympic sprinter. You need capabilities for:

1. **Exceptional Speed:** Cover short to medium distances at high velocity.
2. **Strength and Power:** Have strong quadriceps, hamstrings, glutes, and calf muscles to generate powerful strides and maintain a fast pace.
3. **Technical Skills:** Master proper running technique, including stride length, arm swing, foot strike, and breathing. Efficient running form maximizes speed and reduces the risk of injury.

Capabilities differentiate a wannabe Olympian from a real one. An Olympic runner shouldn't build the capability to bench press more than prime Arnold Schwarzenegger—that's just extra muscle to lug around with each step.

Your capabilities are *how* you create your moats. Take two people with the same how-to-win strategy; the person who develops the right capabilities will always win. Ask yourself: What do we need to be fantastic at to build our moats? Commit to developing two to three capabilities to support each.

For example, Paubox is going to win with their incredible customer service. To do that, they need the capability to offer incredible support at all times, in all forms, to all users.

Drill it down further by asking three additional questions:

1. What new capabilities do we need to develop?
2. What existing capabilities do we need to double down on?
3. What existing capabilities are no longer needed?

That last question is the toughest. It's never easy letting team members go when their capabilities are no longer essential.

Yet if you hold onto them, you're carrying around extra weight you no longer need. In the long-term, you're also doing them a disservice by keeping talent that could thrive in another environment. Everyone deserves a work environment in which their capabilities shine.

Your Turn (To Fill In)

Core Capabilities

Let's tie everything together with a few supplementary strategic choices.

Supplemental Strategic Choices

These choices paint the middle of a bullseye bright red, so it's obvious where to focus.

Most people think of very tactical decisions like, "test our Meta Ads." That's not a strategic choice. A strategic choice that supports that tactical decision might be to double down on Meta as the core marketing channel.

The difference? The latter involves saying no to other marketing channels. Strategic choices are all about what to say "no" to. One of the easiest ways to finalize your strategic choices is to go through these three questions from the Bullseye Strategy Framework.

1. What strategic choices must you make based on your where-to-play strategy?

Each customer you target outside your where-to-play strategy distracts your team. I was helping a leadership team develop their where-to-play strategy, and we decided to focus on SMBs. Yet the CEO kept signing enterprise customers because they paid the big bucks.

When I talked with the team, they told me those enterprise customers generated 95% of the support issues and took up 90% of the development time because of custom contracts. Without knowing it, the CEO was sabotaging his company.

Eventually, the CEO decided to stop signing enterprise deals that required custom development work so the business could focus on the fast-growing SMB market.

2. What strategic choices must you make to double down on your how-to-win strategy?

To lean into your three moats, what do you need to double down on or say no to?

Paubox has a Differentiation Moat based on its patented IP for sending encrypted emails. They made the strategic choice to lead with marketing their email suite, rather than forms or texting products.

3. What strategic choices must you make to achieve your 1-Year Picture?

Should you kill certain initiatives? Do you need to reallocate resources to fund your new strategy? You might cut certain capabilities to invest in new ones.

Your strategic choices become your anchor when new initiatives pop up. There's no ambiguity about where to focus, and you can make decisions much more quickly.

Your Turn (To Fill In)

Supplemental Strategic Choices

Rolling Out Your Winning Strategy

Creating your strategy is the easy part.

Rolling it out is the hard part. As James A. Robinson and Daron Acemoglu detail in *Why Nations Fail,* any new change requires creative destruction.

Let there be creative destruction.

If you don't shake up your business, someone else will. All businesses that last more than a decade need to cannibalize themselves and reinvest profits from the core product into a different future.

As Jason Fried, founder of 37Signals, shared with me on the ProductLed Podcast, the CEO's main job is to introduce risk into the business. Everyone else's job is to manage and mitigate that risk.

Your strategy is nothing more than a theory on how you're going to win. If you have 100% confidence, you waited too long. Your competitors know it, too.

Get the rest of your team aligned on your strategy. The first step is to put it all together in a one-pager. We call this a One-Page Endgame (OPE).

One-Page Endgame (OPE)

Company Name:

Designed by:

Date:

Obvious Choice

Ideal Customer

Core Problem

Primary Marketing Channel(s)

Core Product

Geography

Moat #1

Moat #2

Moat #3

Endgame

Core Values

1-Year Picture

Quarterly Picture

Monthly Picture

Core Capabilities

Strategic Choices

Download a virtual copy here

Based on the book The Product-Led Playbook: How to Unlock Self-Serve Revenue and Dominate Your Market (With a Tiny Team)

ProductLed®
productled.com

Share your OPE with everyone who:

- Has to act on it.
- Will be affected by changes in it.
- Could offer valuable feedback.

Your OPE is a high-level overview of the direction of your business. Explain how you arrived at the strategy and how your business will change.

Action Tool: One-Page Endgame (OPE) Canvas

Head on over to ProductLedPlaybook.com and download your one-page endgame template. Use it to communicate to the rest of the team what the strategy is, how and why you arrived at it, and its implications.

Download a virtual copy here.

Finally, be sure to review it frequently. We'll cover exactly how to do this in the Process Component.

While a winning strategy is a critical component to a successful product-led motion, even the best strategies underperform without a deep understanding of your ideal user.

Actionable Takeaways

- A well-defined strategy provides a clear direction and aligns the entire team's efforts toward a common goal. Trying to do everything dilutes efforts, saps resources, and diminishes results.
- Moats create a competitive advantage that makes your business hard to copy.
- If you're playing to win, everyone must understand your endgame.
- Building the right capabilities ensures you can support your chosen moats.
- Regular communication and review of your strategy keeps it relevant and aligns the entire team.

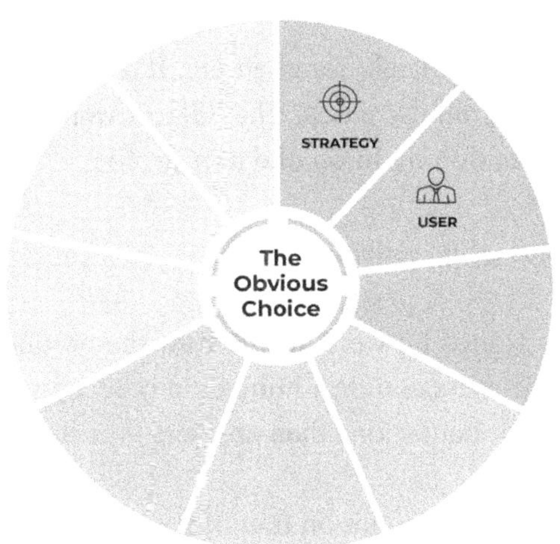

Ideal User

Do you understand your ideal user better than anyone else in your market?

Undefined Ideal User   Average User Intimacy   Deep User Intimacy

Rate yourself from 1 to 10.

Whoever knows the customer best wins the market.

Your primary objective? Get laser-focused on who you're serving.

When you don't, the cost will be steep.

Building for everyone equals building for NO ONE.

Take ProductLed client LucidLink, for example. It's a storage collaboration platform with many potential use cases. They didn't want to exclude potential users and were shy about honing in on one user profile.

So, they kept their messaging general.

As a result, users who signed up were unsure how the product could best help them. Even best-fit users couldn't immediately recognize its value. Generalization led to more questions than answers—as it usually does.

LucidLink fell into the all-too-common trap of trying to be everything to everybody. Here's what happens when you don't make the strategic sacrifice to cater to one user profile:

- It's hard to understand how to serve users better.
- Deciding what to give away for free in your product-led model is difficult.
- You weaken your offer by trying to speak to too many users simultaneously.
- Your onboarding becomes chaotic with so many use cases.
- Your pricing becomes confusing as users all see value differently.
- You have a high churn rate.

When LucidLink made the switch to focus on one user profile group (media production companies), it saw a massive uptick in users. Not only did they see a 40% increase in signups, but their entire team aligned on helping these specific users succeed.

Success starts with a strong understanding of your users. Problem is, most companies have a weak sense of who their users *really* are.

Why is that?

Treating Buyers and Users as Equals

Let's clarify a crucial distinction. Users interact with your product while buyers make the purchasing decision.

For direct-to-consumer businesses, these roles often overlap; a user buys *and* uses the product. If you sign up for a simple application like Chess.com, play a few chess games, and decide to purchase it, you are both the user and the buyer.

However, in many B2B scenarios, the buyer and user are different people. The buyer could be a C-suite executive, while the users are buried further down the organizational hierarchy.

If you focus solely on the buyer's needs, you may create a product that buyers appreciate but users despise. This scenario leads to poor adoption, as users—who interact with the product daily—find it clunky or ineffective. On the other hand, if you focus on creating a product that users love, they will advocate for it, secure budgets, or even make personal purchases.

The Importance of Identifying an "Ideal User"

Not all users are created equal. An ideal user thrives with your solution, engaging with it regularly, sharing it with others, upgrading without hesitation, and providing valuable feedback. These users are easy to serve and often become your biggest advocates.

You can spot ideal users by looking at which customers use the product the most, upgrade the quickest, and leave the best testimonials.

When you become maniacal about helping your ideal user, you'll see:

- **Enhanced product-market fit**. Tailoring the product to a specific user ensures it meets their needs perfectly, making it more likely that they will choose and stick with the product.
- **Efficient resource allocation**: Instead of spreading efforts thinly across multiple user types, businesses can concentrate on developing features and services that significantly benefit their ideal user.

- **Effective marketing and messaging**: Clarity in messaging better resonates with the target user, leading to higher engagement and conversion rates.
- **Stronger user loyalty and advocacy**: When a product is designed to meet the specific needs of a particular user, they are more enthusiastic about the product and more likely to recommend it to others.

When you focus on an ideal user, you get to know them better than anyone else in the market. You know their deepest challenges and focus all your energy on serving them.

The User Endgame Roadmap Model

You can narrow down who your ideal user is, understand their unique challenges, and learn how to design a product experience that powers your bottom-up sales motion with the User Endgame Roadmap Model.

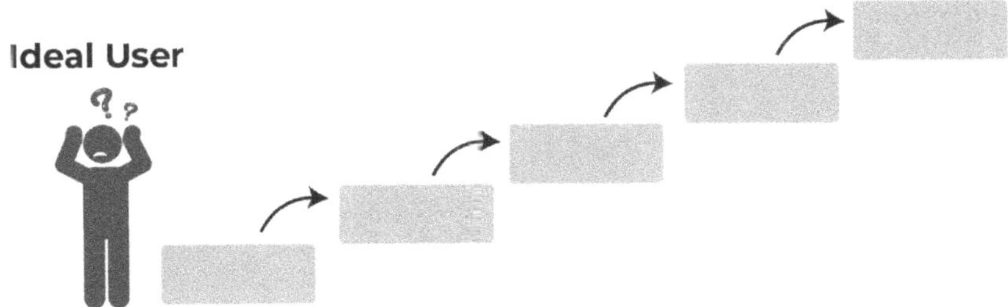

Phase 1: Identify Your Ideal User

Every product attracts an Ideal User Profile (IUP). ClickUp appeals to productivity enthusiasts, while Netflix targets entertainment lovers. Your business is no different.

To find this user, you must understand what makes them "ideal":

1. **Love your product:** Are enthusiastic about the product and excited to use it, even if the product still needs improvement.
2. **Great Retention:** Tend to stick around for a long time and gain substantial value from the product.
3. **Highly Successful:** Derive more value from the product than other users due to their specific use cases and technical skills, which maximize the product's potential.
4. **Strategic:** Help you break into the market more effectively, as they are often looked up to by others, increasing awareness and credibility.

I've seen too many companies try to focus on two, three, or even four ideal users. The most common justification is that they have a horizontal product that can appeal to many users. Although that's true, only a small subsection of people really care about what your product does.

You want to build a product for your ideal users because they're the ones who will become your raving fans. Raving fans bring more fans to your door. (How did you hear of Canva? *From a raving fan.*)

Olly Meakings runs Senja.io, a software application that makes it easy to collect and share testimonials. Senja is a horizontal application; many different users can get value out of the product.

When Olly was defining his ideal user, he listed three options:

1. SaaS founders
2. Freelance writers
3. Course creators

Olly's intuition was to serve the SaaS founders. However, when he spoke to other SaaS founders, he learned they weren't that motivated to use the product and noted alternatives like G2, Capterra, and Trustpilot.

When Olly analyzed each group (more on that later), he noticed that course creators were the most motivated and saw it as a vital tool in their marketing toolkit.

Senja.io had all the features a course creator could ever dream of, while SaaS founders would insist on more integrations. Olly knew he could scale well past $1M ARR by focusing solely on course creators.

Your ideal users should love your product for what it is *right now.*

Step 1: Write Down as Many Ideal Users as You Can

Start by listing potential ideal users. For B2B SaaS businesses, these are often job titles. Don't aim for perfection.

Remember, a buyer is not always the user. If you're selling a marketing automation product, the VP of Demand Generation (i.e., the buyer) might purchase it, but the Digital Marketing Specialist is the user.

Potential Ideal Users (To Fill In)

Once you've listed five to ten potential ideal users, it's time to narrow it down.

Step 2: Identify a User's Likelihood of Success

Assess each user's likelihood of success using three key indicators from the BJ Fogg Behavior Model:

1. **Motivation:** They're extremely motivated to use the product—something is pushing or pulling them in this direction.
2. **Ability:** It's relatively easy for them to pick up and use the product (e.g., maybe they have programming experience).
3. **Prompts:** It's top-of-mind. They're constantly getting triggers to fix this problem, whether internal or external.

As long as a user has enough motivation, ability, and prompts, they can achieve any target behavior—including success in your product.

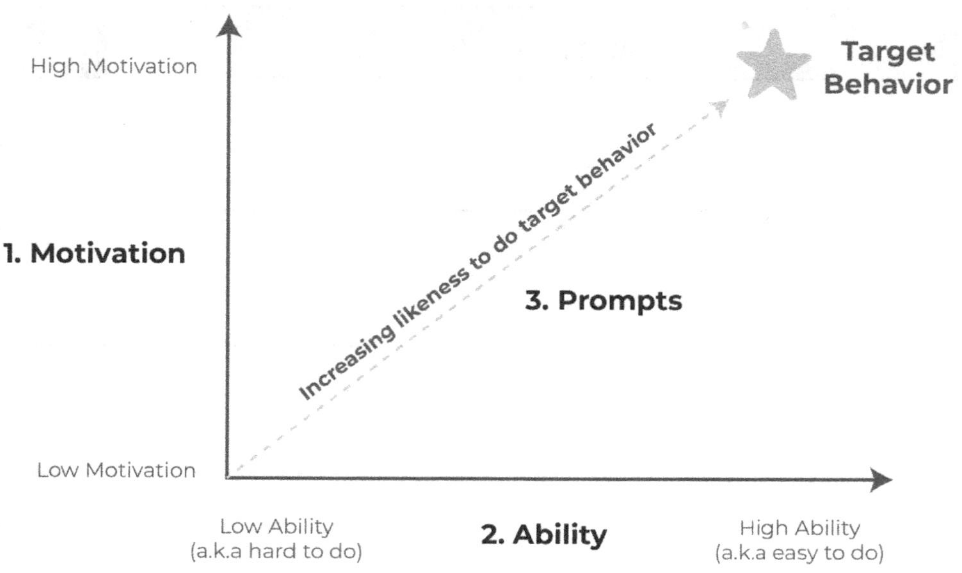

For example, developers are more likely to succeed than marketers with a highly technical application. I'm more likely to workout consistently if I do workouts that I enjoy, such as swimming. And you're more likely to read this book if I don't overwhelm you with too much all at once.

Rate each potential ideal user based on these three key indicators.

Potential Ideal Users	Motivation	Ability	Prompts
SaaS Founders	Somewhat Motivated	Easy	Strong Prompts
Course Creators	Highly Motivated	Easy	Strong Prompts
Freelance Writers	Not Motivated	Difficult	No Prompts

Your Turn (To Fill In)

Potential Ideal Users	Motivation	Ability	Prompts

You'll start seeing a trend—one or two users reach the top. Still, you might not want to pick the top one.

For example, ProductLed client Kloudle is up against many bigger, better-funded players going after security engineers. The security engineer's full-time job is to find and fix security issues. They're the most motivated, have the highest ability, and get tons of prompts to address security issues.

Yet, the founder, Akash, didn't pick this ideal user. For one, it was saturated. Second, it didn't lean into their strengths as a business. Kloudle is unique because it automatically identifies security issues without needing expensive security engineers.

So, he decided to target smaller companies where a developer is tasked with solving security issues. This user isn't as motivated to solve this issue, but they know it has to be done. They could set everything up and use internal prompts to fix them. Sounds lackluster, but what makes Kloudle stand out is that the product could find and fix most security issues automatically—music to your ears if you don't want to do something.

Akash knows his ideal user has super limited motivation, so he created a product that was the quick fix his ideal user wanted.

If you're finding it difficult to narrow down your ideal user, add additional columns:

1. TAM: Is the total addressable market big enough?
2. Free-to-paid conversion rate: Do ideal users convert at a higher rate?
3. Retention Rate: Do ideal users stick around the longest?

Use this framework to identify who will be the most successful with your product and make a compelling case for why you'll focus on them.

The next step is to commit to just one.

Step 3: Identify One Ideal User

I've seen so many SaaS founders analyze this to death. Too many companies take too long to double down, which lengthens the learning curve.

Of course, you want to get as much research and data as possible to back up your decision. Still, you'll never have enough to decide with 100% accuracy. And if you do, you've spent too much time and energy trying to get it right.

Colin Powell, the former U.S. Secretary of State, had a 40 to 70 rule: Without 40% of the available information, you'll make a bad choice; with more than 70%, you'll have waited too long—and the choice will be made for you.

But how do you know if you're closer to 40 or 70? Ask three questions:

1. Use your head brain: "Who do I *think* is the right ideal user for our business?" Use logic and data to determine the ideal user. Analyze data, understand market trends, and make a business case.
2. Use your heart brain: "Who do I *feel* is the right ideal user for our business?" Tap into your intuition and emotional intelligence. Align the choice with what feels inherently right for the business and its values.
3. Use your gut brain: "Who do I *have the courage* to say is our ideal user?" Commit to a specific user segment, even if it excludes others. Take a bold stand and focus resources on this group.

You make better decisions when you use your three brains. You can read more about the science behind it in *mBraining* by Grant Soosalu and Marvin Oka.

Getting it "right" the first time can feel overwhelming. Still, pick one. Refine it as you get more data and insight to validate that it is, in fact, the "ideal" user.

The first time we did this activity at ProductLed, we picked the wrong ideal user. We first chose Senior Product Executives. But we soon realized that it's difficult for them to be successful at PLG when it isn't adopted by the CEO, who makes it a company-wide initiative. Only then did we make the call to focus on founders and CEOs.

Your ideal user will evolve as you scale your business. You may even find that you've maxed out one segment and are ready to move on to the next—that's great!

When you finally identify the right ideal user, you'll know. Customers will be easier to serve, you'll make more revenue per customer, and conversions will increase as you double down.

The challenge is sticking with your thesis long enough to identify some of those positive signals. How long? There's no definitive answer. But if you're seeing bad conversion rates, low referability, and bad retention, it might be time to move on to the next user profile.

So pick one ideal user, especially if this is your first time going through the ProductLed System. Even if you add just one more ideal user, you'll lose focus. You'll learn the most from picking one and serving them.

Once you've done that, it's time to clarify the endgame for your ideal user.

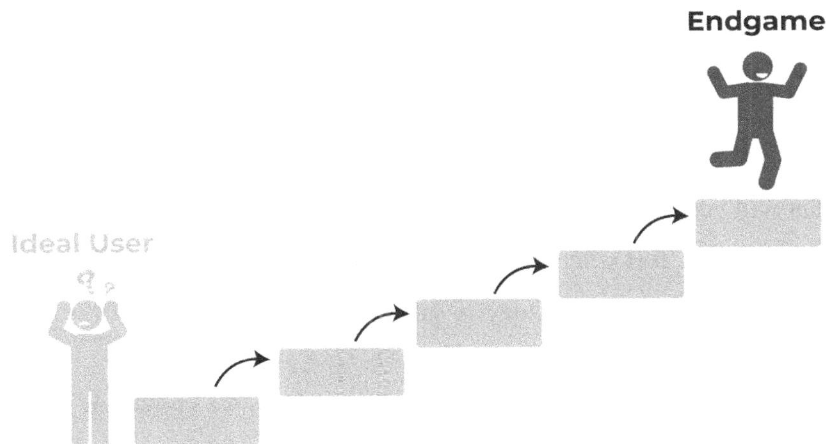

Phase 2: Clarify the Endgame

What is a user capable of once they experience the value of your product?

When you play *Super Mario Bros.* and pick up a flower, Mario grows bigger and can spew fire—he's a complete badass.

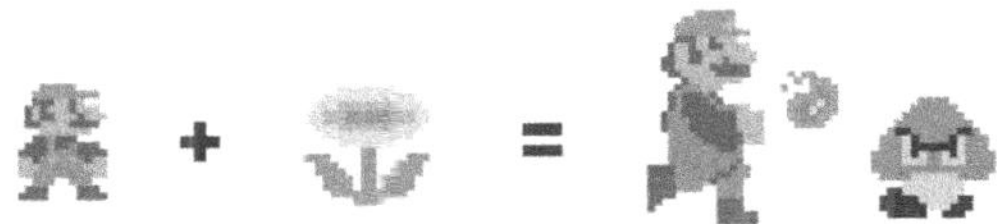

Your product is the flower. That badass version of Mario is a successful user.

Too often, companies obsess over their product yet don't pay attention to how many fire-spewing Marios they create.

Let's change that!

Step 1: List All Core Outcomes

When your users are successful, what core outcomes will they experience?

These three questions can get your wheels spinning:

1. What will your users **see** when they're successful?
2. What will they **feel** when they're successful?
3. What will they **hear** when they're successful?

For example, if you implement the ProductLed System, we know you'll experience three core outcomes:

1. Effortless ARR: Your product will sell itself.
2. Lean Scale: You'll be able to scale without hiring a big team.
3. Durable Growth: Your business will be profitable over the long-term.

Everything we do in this book and in our implementation program helps you achieve those core outcomes.

List out all the potential outcomes your product helps users with. Keep it simple.

Your Turn (To Fill In)

Example Outcomes	Potential Outcomes (To Fill In)
Enhanced Customer Testimonials	
Increased Conversion Rates	
Centralized Management	
Versatile Sharing Options	

Step 2: Pinpoint Your Top 3 Outcomes

Hone in on the top three outcomes your product delivers. Typically, these involve:

1. **Fix:** Immediate problems or pain.
2. **Prevent**: Fear of missing out, or harm.
3. **Improve**: Long-term gain or advantage.

Don't feel limited by these suggestions; outcomes come in different forms. The key is to simplify your description of how you help users win.

Your Turn (To Fill In)

Core Outcomes

Once you've nailed your outcomes, do the last step and define your user endgame statement.

Step 3: Define Your User Endgame Statement

Your user endgame statement communicates what the end transformation looks like. Your top three outcomes should directly support it.

At ProductLed, we define this as becoming “the obvious choice in your market.”

This is the big transformation we want you to make. You’re no longer a commodity. Your company stands out and is the leading option in the market.

Here are some examples of user endgame statements:

1. Canva: Design anything and publish anywhere.
2. Hotjar: Get insights to create digital experiences your users love.
3. Google: Find relevant answers to any question.
4. Shopify: Build your dream business.
5. Zapier: Automate your busy work.

It should meet the following criteria:

- ☐ It communicates what it’s not.
- ☐ It inspires.
- ☐ It’s simple to understand.
- ☐ It’s achievable.
- ☐ Your product can deliver on it.

When it checks all of the boxes, you’re close.

A user endgame statement is a one-liner that’s easy to communicate to your team. It aligns your team on what it means when your user succeeds.

Fill out your statement below.

User Endgame Statement

Now that you've clarified what the endgame is, it's time to map out the user journey to see what prevents them from reaching it.

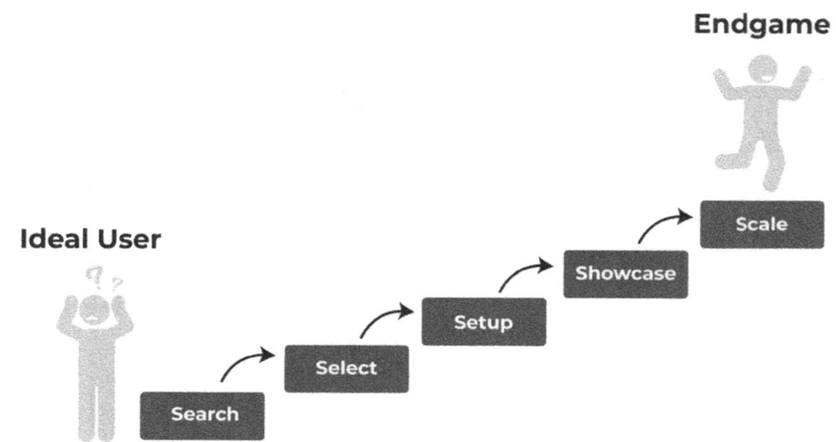

Phase 3: Craft a User Roadmap

A user roadmap helps you understand the exact steps a user must take to get value from your product. Companies without a roadmap tend to pay for it with a low percentage of users who reach value and an equally abysmal upgrade rate.

Most users won't make it through the entire user roadmap. That's okay. There are five main stages. Each has two milestones to help users progress through their journey.

Search Stage

In the Search Stage, users have two big milestones:

1. **Problem Aware:** They realize they have a problem.
2. **Active Research:** They conduct active research on how to solve the problem.

Challenges include information overload, fear of change, and limited knowledge of how to solve the problem. If you're in a commoditized space, users will move on pretty quickly from this step. But if it's a new problem, they might do more research.

Educating users at this stage is crucial. If you know what their biggest challenges are, you can educate them on how to think about how to solve the problem.

Here are some examples of common challenges users face at this stage.

Problem Aware	Active Research
Information overload	Cost concerns
Fear of change	Technical jargon
Complacency	Integration concerns
Limited knowledge	Security and privacy challenges

It's your job to educate users on the root problem before they solve the wrong problem in a non-ideal way.

Your Turn (To Fill In)

Problem Aware	Active Research

Next is the Select Stage, where they learn more about your product.

Select Stage

In the Select Stage, users learn about your solution and decide whether to sign up.

It breaks down into two milestones:

1. **Visit:** Visiting your website.
2. **Sign Up:** Signing up for your free product.

Here are some examples of common challenges users might encounter:

Visit	Sign Up
Website navigation issues	Unclear benefits of signing up
Too many calls-to-action	Too many form fields
Overwhelming amount of information	Technical issues
Slow loading speeds	Mandatory credit card signup
Unresponsive design	Concerns about privacy and security
Unclear value proposition	Uncertainty about free trial or freemium limitations
Lack of trust indicators	Confusing pricing

Screen recording tools can be very helpful here. They observe how visitors interact with your site and help you identify the main challenges.

Your Turn (To Fill In)

Visit	Sign Up

Once users have signed up, they move to the Setup Stage.

Setup Stage

At this point, the clock is ticking for you to deliver value. Your user has a finite amount of energy, time, and motivation to invest in your product.

In an ideal world, a user can sign up and almost instantly start receiving value. But that's rarely the case, especially in B2B. Two milestones can improve your odds of successful setup:

1. **Profile:** Ask your users a few questions to accelerate onboarding.
2. **Onboarding:** Walk them through exactly what they need to do to get value.

What's a profile step? It's a few questions you ask right after your user signs up so that you can serve them better. Typically, this involves asking the user about their goal and collecting more information about their business.

For example, Wave is a financial management tool. When someone signs up, they're asked a few questions about their business and what they'd like to achieve with the platform. Wave then customizes the dashboard and shows them relevant features to get them to value as fast as possible.

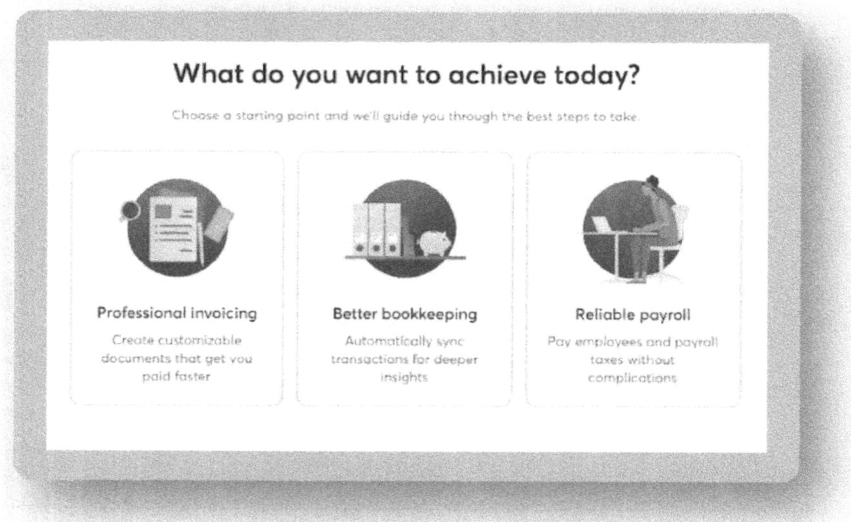

If you don't have this step yet, don't worry. You'll add it in the Onboarding Component to understand what percentage of signups are actually ideal users. Once your user completes the profiling step, you can kick off onboarding.

The onboarding milestone guides users through the initial setup to help them quickly realize the value of your product. Most companies don't design an intentional onboarding experience and lose 40 to 60% of signups at this stage.

Here are some of the most common challenges at the Setup Stage:

Profile	Onboarding
Question survey fatigue	Complex installation process
Unclear purpose	Unclear instructions/guidance
Privacy concerns	Overwhelming amount of features
Language and accessibility issues	Lack of customization
Lack of immediate benefit	Time-consuming process
Technical issues	Insufficient support and resources (e.g., knowledge base, live chat)

Your Turn (To Fill In)

Profile	Onboarding

After onboarding, it's time for users to reach the core value of your product.

Showcase Stage

Once users complete the Setup Stage, they should be ready to experience the product's value. This is straightforward for some products, like Netflix—just start watching. In most B2B SaaS companies, there's a lot more to it.

We divide the Showcase Stage into two milestones:

1. **First Strike:** Experiencing the core value of the product for the first time.
2. **Key Usage Indicator (KUI):** Experiencing the core value multiple times.

The First Strike in your product should empower users—just like Mario with his flower.

A few examples of First Strikes are:

1. Creating your first graphic in Canva.
2. Having your first call on Zoom.
3. Watching your first movie on Netflix.
4. Playing your first chess game on Chess.com.

A First Strike doesn't mean someone has experienced the *entire* value of your product. They've simply received enough value to motivate them to come back. A great First Strike delivers significant value while leaving room for further discovery.

What's the First Strike for your product?

First Strike

Once they've hit the First Strike, be on the lookout for the true sign you've got a user hooked—they come back for more. This is where Key Usage Indicators (KUIs) come in.

Before I sat down to write this paragraph, I had a peanut butter and chocolate energy ball. I had one before I ate my breakfast and put it back in the fridge, but five minutes after breakfast, I had another one. That's a KUI that I love these little energy balls.

Your product should have the same effect. The First Strike is that first yummy energy ball. Then the KUI is eating that second energy ball. Once your users experience the KUI, they're far more likely to develop a habit.

Many times, the KUI is simply experiencing that same First Strike three or more times. Here are a few examples from well-known brands:

- For Slack, a KUI is when an account reaches its 2,000 message limit.
- For Facebook, it's once someone adds seven friends.

A KUI is a great leading indicator that identifies who is getting meaningful value from your product and who is more likely to upgrade.

What does a KUI look like for your product?

Key Usage Indicator (KUI)

The common challenges at this step fall into three buckets:

1. **Product Gap:** Users might need help with the product itself, such as poor user experience or a difficult onboarding process.
2. **Knowledge Gap:** Users lack the necessary knowledge to use the product—it has a high learning curve.
3. **Skill Gap:** Some products require a certain level of skill. If users lack these skills, they may not fully benefit from (or be motivated to use) the product.

As you think through challenges, ask yourself:

1. What challenges do users **see**?
2. What challenges do users **feel**?
3. What challenges do users **hear**?

Here are some of the most common challenges at the Showcase Stage:

First Strike	KUI
Unable to find what they're looking for	External trigger fatigue (they're bombarded with such as emails, SMS texts, and notifications).
Distractions	Overwhelmed with new information
Product bugs	Trust issues
Lack of personalization	No quick reward (e.g., results take 15 minutes)

Your Turn (To Fill In)

First Strike	KUI

Once you've showcased the value of your product, it's time to scale.

Scale Stage

This is the most commonly measured stage that founders obsess over. Are people upgrading?

There are two milestones:

1. **Upgrade**: When users upgrade to a paid plan.
2. **Advance**: When users grow out of their existing plan or simply use your solution more.

The upgrade step is self-explanatory: the user pays for your product. What's not so self-explanatory is *why* your user decides to upgrade.

Take the word "upgrade" literally. What is the user looking to upgrade in their life? This isn't about features—it's accomplishing something meaningful. The answer should be compelling to users and solve a genuine problem they care about. It should also be sequential.

For instance, Senja's free plan makes it easy to collect testimonials. However, every testimonial is still branded with "Powered by Senja." As business owners become more established, many want to showcase a more professional experience, so they upgrade to a paid plan that eliminates the Senja branding.

What needs to be true for it to be a no-brainer for your users to upgrade?

Once they've upgraded, you need to continue delivering value.

The advance milestone empowers users to continue to get more value and justify the upgrade. In some businesses, users adopt the product as part of their workflow (e.g., Canva, Miro, or Notion). For other products, this step looks like a user completing everything they need to experience its full value.

In an ideal world, you'll grow with your users, but that's not always true. Some users "graduate" and seek out more advanced solutions. Others will collaborate with you to build out advanced features. Either way, you need to co-develop the advanced milestone with your customers to build out the next edition of your product. The endgame is making customers wildly successful, raving fans.

Here are the most common user challenges at the Scale Stage:

Upgrade	Advance
Confusing pricing	Steep learning curve
Inadequate free experience	Prohibitive pricing
Payment issues	Integration difficulties
Unclear cancellation policy	Inadequate customization
Limited payment options	Performance issues
Migration concerns	Lack of advanced tutorials or community support
Support concerns	Team adoption

Your Turn (To Fill In)

Upgrade	Advance

At this stage, you need to be highly innovative and tap into what your customers want. Otherwise, it's only a matter of time before the competition catches up and you lose your best customers.

User Endgame Canvas

Company Name:

Designed by:

Date:

Ideal User	Core Outcomes	User Endgame

Search	Select	Setup	Showcase	Scale
Top Challenges	Top Challenges	Top Challenges	First Strike	Top Challenges
			Key Usage Indicator	
			Top Challenges	

Download a virtual copy here

Based on the book The Product-Led Playbook: How to Unlock Self-Serve Revenue and Dominate Your Market (With a Tiny Team)

productled.com

Honing in on Your Ideal User

The User Endgame Roadmap helps you get clarity around who your ideal user is, what success means for them, and identifies their biggest roadblocks.

If you implement the User Endgame Roadmap, you'll get to know your users better than anyone else in your market. Here's the User Endgame Canvas for you to fill out with your team.

Action Tool: User Endgame Canvas

Head on over to ProductLedPlaybook.com and download a copy of the User Endgame Canvas. Use it to get to know your user better than anyone else.

Download a virtual copy here.

But here's the deal. This isn't a set-it-and-forget-it activity. Your ideal user will change over time. Your user's endgame might change based on new technology. Their challenges will evolve as you solve the initial ones and understand them better.

Although the activities we've outlined are highly effective at getting leadership teams on the same page about your ideal user and what impedes their success, nothing replaces actually talking to customers.

Get out there and become the leading expert on your ideal users.

Actionable Takeaways

- By tailoring your product to a specific user, you ensure it meets their needs perfectly, leading to higher adoption and retention.
- Focusing on one ideal user allows you to develop features and services that significantly benefit them, maximizing your impact.
- Clear messaging that resonates with your ideal user leads to higher engagement and conversion rates.
- A product designed for specific user needs generates enthusiastic users who are more likely to recommend it to others.

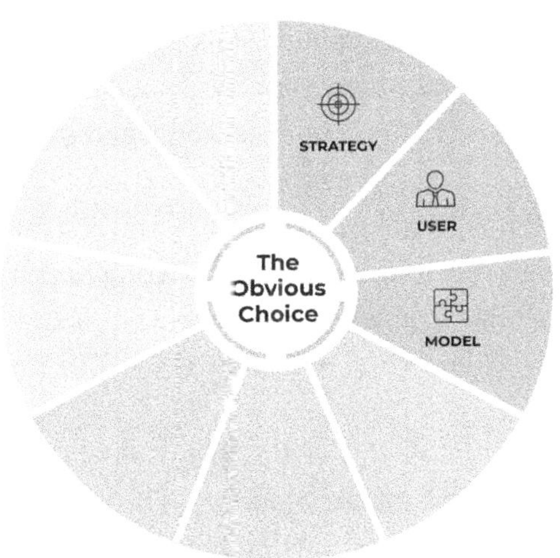

Intentional Model

How **intentional** is your free model?

We Guessed — Mediocre Model — Perfectly Free

Rate yourself from 1 to 10.

A product-led model determines what to give away for free and what to charge for. The best product-led models give users everything they need to succeed at each stage of their user journey.

Yet, designing a product-led model is hard. Even if you understand your users well, you can still get your model wrong.

Take Tettra as an example. Tettra is an online knowledge base for your team that makes it easy to create and share important documents like your time-off policy. They initially had a 15-day free trial model and found it hard to scale the business.

They had relatively high short-term churn and mediocre conversion rates across the board. Why? Because what could users do in 15 days with an online knowledge-based tool? Would you invest time and effort if you knew you had only 15 days to use it?

Tettra couldn't shine with their free-trial model. The real value kicked in when companies built up a trove of important company documents over time to train employees. Without knowing it, Tettra had created a product-led model that prioritized asking for money before providing value.

On the other hand, a freemium model could provide more value upfront, give users time to set up their knowledge base, and allow Tettra to ask for money when the time is right. So Tettra pivoted to freemium. It worked.

The freemium model allowed users to try the product without a time limit. In addition, Tettra didn't ask for credit card information, which led to more people onboarding, finding value, and converting. While more "tire kickers" drained some resources, that was a manageable problem with automation, and the increase in signups outweighed the losses.

Upgrades increased, too. While Tettra expected Monthly Recurring Revenue (MRR) to go down, the number of upgrades counteracted the drop: The freemium switch tripled the number of upgrades by the 5th quarter.

What about retention? After the freemium launch, it never dipped below 70% and consistently had 100% retention rates throughout the year.[9]

When you identify the *right* product-led model, good things happen. It's easier to scale. It's easier to convert users into paying customers. It's easier to keep customers.

Yet, if you can believe it, **there is no single correct model.** Multi-billion dollar product-led companies have made PLG work with free trials, freemium models, reverse trials, and other free models. You can find a company that has made every model work.

What goes into the model matters more than the model itself.

An intentional product-led model solves a meaningful problem for users. Sometimes, that takes days; other times, it takes months. The biggest challenge is deciding what goes into the model and ensuring that your product's true value can shine in your free motion.

The Three Common Scenarios

When signing up for a product-led model, you'll likely run into three scenarios.

The first is the most common expectation—the free product gives you a new capability. You'll grow 2X bigger. You'll spew fire, just like Mario.

You're aiming for that gold standard.

Most times, however, a second scenario occurs. You pick up the free model but are exactly the same.

What do you do? Most ditch the product and never return.

Now, the third, least common scenario happens mostly with VC-backed companies. They can often afford to forgo monetizing users in pursuit of aggressive user-growth targets. So what do they do?

They give away almost *everything* for free, removing the motivation to upgrade—you can beat the game with your new, no-cost abilities.

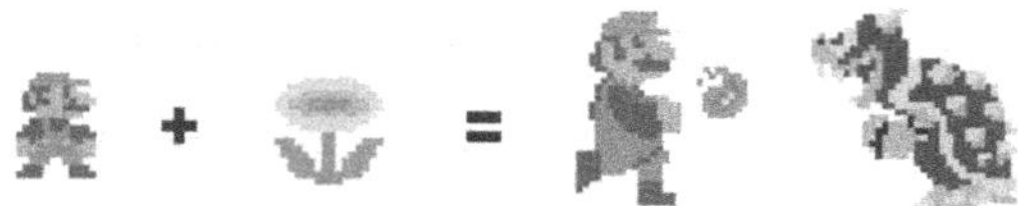

That's how I used Evernote for eight lovely years before paying them a dime. I had zero reason to upgrade until they finally dumbed down their free model (more on that story later).

So, what's the goal of *your* free model? It should be to give your users everything they need to tackle a big, hairy problem they couldn't solve on their own.

It's not about letting them beat the game—it's helping them level up.

What scenario best represents your free model?

The goal is to build enough trust with your users to show you can deliver on your promise.

Let's see how to do just that with the DEEP model.

Phase 1: Desirable – Gamify Your Model Into Three Levels

Think of your free model as a game. Every game has levels—some version of beginner, intermediate, and advanced.

In a product-led business, each level equates to a key step in your user's journey. Your job is to break down the full user journey into those levels and make it easy for users to advance from one to the next.

If you don't do this, you might run into the Cold Start Problem—starting to solve advanced problems in your free motion before addressing beginner problems.

When I worked at Vidyard, we encountered this issue. This was why our initial free trial was unsuccessful. At the time, Vidyard was known for video marketing analytics. You could know exactly what percentage of a video someone watched on your website. Creepy, but cool!

To see the value of our video marketing analytics during our free trial, you'd have to:

1. Upload a video to the platform.
2. Embed that video on your website.
3. Integrate Vidyard with your marketing automation platform.
4. Drive traffic to the page with the video.
5. And voila! You could see who's watching your videos.

How many users completed all of these steps? Next to none. It wasn't hard to do, and the platform wasn't clunky. The real problem was that we were solving an advanced problem. Most users didn't even have a video to upload.

So, we launched a simple Chrome extension that made it easy to record a video with a few clicks. You could easily send it to anyone, and when they watched it, you'd see what percentage of the video they watched.

This solved a beginner problem. That Chrome extension took off, gaining 100,000+ users in the first 12 months—and millions of users since then.

When designing your game, take a step back. Remind yourself what the ultimate user endgame is and break it down into three levels.

A beginner level represents a problem that everyone in your market would need help with at some point. This is what you'll give away for free. Don't worry yet about the specifics of what you'll give away—just focus on the desired outcome.

An intermediate level represents a problem that most of your market will eventually struggle with. The advanced level represents a problem that only a minority of the market struggles with.

Each level has a desired outcome. Once users experience the outcome of one level, they can continue at their current level or graduate to the next one. In the Vidyard example, a user can start making videos easily at the beginner level, so they feel confident making these videos and using them in sales.

Eventually, the number of videos they can create will be limited. At this point, they can upgrade to the next level, unlock unlimited videos, and access more features to help them sell more.

Once a user is extremely successful using Vidyard, they might roll this out to their entire team so that they can all use video to sell more.

User Endgame: Wow your buyers and win more deals		
Beginner Level	**Intermediate Level**	**Advanced Level**
Beginner Outcome: Start recording and sharing videos easily.	**Intermediate Outcome:** Unlock unlimited videos and make more sales.	**Advanced Outcome:** Level up your entire team's sales game with videos.

The transition from one level to another is seamless—just what we're going for.

I'll share one more example. Among ProductLed's clients is PromoTix, an event ticketing platform similar to Eventbrite. For them, the user endgame is hosting a sold-out event with happy attendees.

The desired outcome of an event host is to publish an event so they can start selling tickets. Once that's done, the goal is to sell out that event. However, to do that, they need powerful marketing tools. That's when it makes sense for them to upgrade to the intermediate level.

If you're selling tons of tickets, you'll run into another issue: ticketing fees start to add up. That's when you'll want to lock in a fixed monthly rate—exactly what's available at the advanced level.

User Endgame: Hosting sold-out events with happy attendees.		
Beginner Level	**Intermediate Level**	**Advanced Level**
Beginner Outcome: Publish an event.	**Intermediate Outcome:** Sell more tickets with marketing tools.	**Advanced Outcome:** Save big on ticketing fees.

Once again, there's a clear progression from beginner to advanced. Don't overcomplicate this by adding too many levels. Most businesses do just fine with three.

For your product, what's a meaningful win that someone could experience in less than seven minutes? That's the beginner level.

One of the most common issues I help ProductLed clients avoid is giving away too much for free. For instance, one of the companies we serve has a coaching platform that allows you to train university students to work as accountants. Their unique ability is that they help learners acquire technical skills fast.

They wanted to give away five courses for free. However, it might take up to a year for companies to set up five courses. So we recommended they give away one free course instead. Remember: the goal here isn't to have free users for life. It's to help them to get to value and upgrade.

Be generous with your beginner level. Give users everything they need to level up. But don't overwhelm them with unnecessary features.

Your beginner outcome should check these boxes:

- Unique: Does my product's unique core value shine?
- Desirable: Does my ideal user *really* want this outcome?
- Effective: Can my ideal user experience the outcome in seven minutes or less?

Remember, no one likes to play a game they can't win or where the odds are stacked against them. If you can't make your free offer desirable, no one will want to play.

Your Turn (To Fill Out)

Endgame:		
Beginner Level	**Intermediate Level**	**Advanced Level**
Beginner Outcome:	**Intermediate Outcome:**	**Advanced Outcome:**

Once you're clear on what the main outcome is for each level, unpack what's stopping your ideal user from reaching those outcomes.

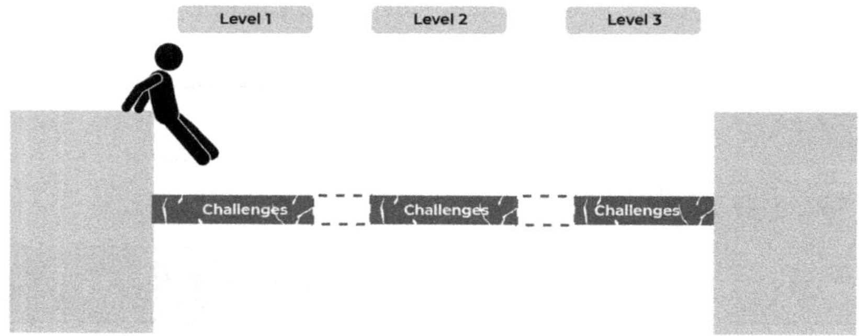

Phase 2: Effective – Unpack the Biggest Challenges

Before you can design the perfect free model for your users, you must understand every challenge they'll face. You'll use that knowledge to give them the right tools.

Thanks to the groundwork you've done in the User Component, this will be relatively easy. Review your User Endgame Roadmap and place the challenges you've identified into their respective levels.

Here's how PromoTix broke down their challenges:

User Endgame: Hosting sold-out events with happy attendees.		
Beginner Level	**Intermediate Level**	**Advanced Level**
Beginner Outcome: Publish an event.	**Intermediate Outcome:** Sell more tickets with marketing tools.	**Advanced Outcome:** Save big on ticketing fees.
Challenges: • Planning the event. • Ticket pricing. • Getting the event set up. • Selling the tickets.	**Challenges:** • Marketing the tickets. • Creating graphics for event promotion. • Recurring event options.	**Challenges:** • Offering VIP experiences, camping passes, additional day passes, merchandise, and add-ons.

• Designing an image for the event page. • Sharing the event page with people.	• Booking talent or artists to boost ticket sales.	• Setting up RFID ticketing. • Season tickets. • Ambassador program that meets the needs of promoters. • Creating a mobile app.

Add new challenges, too. You can use AI tools to brainstorm challenges to achieve a desired outcome. Use a prompt like "List out the biggest challenges for [Ideal User] to achieve [Desired Outcome]." You'll be surprised how accurate the results are. It's not a comprehensive list, but it'll break through writer's block.

Most challenges fall into three buckets:

1. Product challenges: How can a user experience the value of your product?
2. Knowledge challenges: What does your user not know that's holding them back?
3. Skill challenges: Which lacking skills prevent success?

One of our ProductLed clients, Userguiding.com, simplifies the process of rolling out tooltips to help guide users more effectively within your application. The product itself is relatively simple to set up. Yet, they need to educate their users a lot and guide them through how to use these tooltips effectively.

Otherwise, they might showcase all the features while their user doesn't accomplish anything meaningful in the product. So many of their challenges relate to a knowledge and skill gap.

Your Turn (To Fill Out)

User Endgame:		
Beginner Level	Intermediate Level	Advanced Level
Beginner Outcome:	**Intermediate Outcome:**	**Advanced Outcome:**
Challenges:	**Challenges:**	**Challenges:**

Identify at least five to 10 challenges for each level. The more, the better, as you'll have a better understanding of what's holding users back.

Prioritize Challenges

Once you're done listing out all your challenges, classify them on the Roadblock Rating from 1 to 5:

1 - It doesn't feel like a challenge (everyone can overcome it).
2 - Small challenge (almost no one has a problem with this).
3 - Decent challenge (many users are pointing out this obstacle).
4 - Most users face this challenge but can't overcome it.
5 - No users can overcome this challenge without support.

You'll quickly start to understand which challenges most impact your users. Tackling some of the biggest challenges first will help more users reach the next level.

Here's what this might look like for the beginner level.

Challenges	Magnitude
Planning the event	4
Ticket pricing	3
Getting the event setup	5
Selling the tickets	4
Designing an image for the event page	1
Sharing the event page with people	3

Once you've identified the magnitude of each challenge, shortlist the ones you'll tackle for each level. This doesn't mean ignoring all other challenges. It does mean focusing on overcoming the top three to five that prevent users from completing a level.

The top three challenges for PromoTix are clear:

1. Get the event set up.
2. Plan the event.
3. Sell the tickets.

Your Turn (To Fill Out)

Challenges	Magnitude

Once you've identified the top three to five challenges, you can arm users with everything they need to succeed at every level.

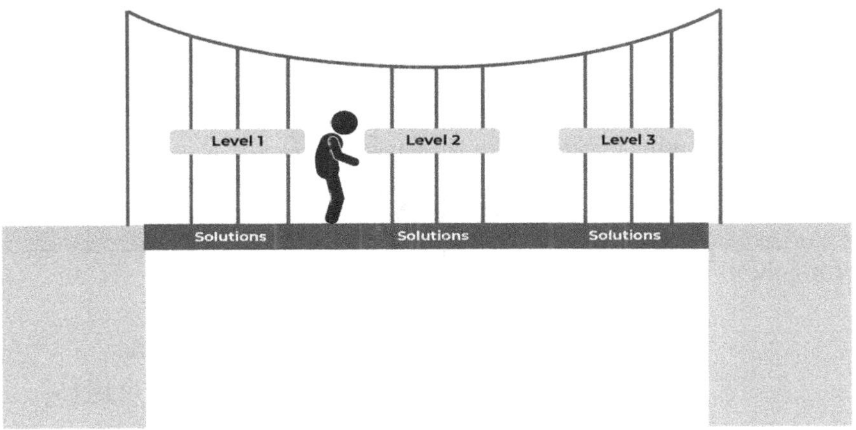

Phase 3: Efficient – Decide What to Give Away for Free and What to Gate

Without the right tools to succeed, users will attempt to move from one level to the next—but they're playing the game on "hard mode."

Your users need "power-ups" (a.k.a. solutions) to avoid or defeat challenges they encounter. The goal is to make each level easy to achieve.

To get started, run the PCR test.

Step 1: Run the PCR Test

Let's say your user's top challenge is to "publish an event page." The PCR test will show you how to find the best solutions for that challenge:

1. Product solutions.
2. Content solutions.
3. Resource solutions.

A content solution is consumed and easy to share; a resource solution is interactive (e.g., quiz).

Instead of just one potential solution for each challenge, you'll want to develop many different ones. For major challenges, that's a great thing. Some people prefer to learn, while others want a dedicated tool.

Here's how this breaks down for PromoTix's beginner level.

<table>
<tr><th colspan="2">Beginner Level</th></tr>
<tr><td colspan="2">Beginner Outcome: Publish an event page</td></tr>
<tr><th>Challenge</th><th>Solutions</th></tr>
<tr><td rowspan="3">Getting the event set up.</td><td>Product Solutions
• Free event page builder.
• Payment processing options.
• Embedded checkout.
• Ticket inventory management.
• Unlimited ticket types.
• Event photo generator.</td></tr>
<tr><td>Content Solutions
• What to include on your event page.
• How to write event descriptions that convert.
• Examples of event pages.</td></tr>
<tr><td>Resource Solutions
• List of the best event page designers.
• 1,000 top venues and who to contact.
• Ticket tier pricing model.</td></tr>
</table>

Ideally, you'll identify at least five to 10 potential solutions for every challenge.

Why so many?

By doing this, you'll identify unique solutions that help your users overcome these challenges easily. This is also another reason why you should do this with your team: you'll unlock creative solutions to complex challenges. One of the issues with brainstorming is it's way too easy to only focus on product solutions.

For instance, if you ask a group of product managers how to help users sell more tickets, you'll hear many product-related solutions. Yet, this challenge could have been addressed with a simple blog post.

Once you've listed out your solutions, you should feel confident that if your users had access to everything, they would easily accomplish each level in your game.

Step 2: Prioritize Your Solutions

In an ideal world, you'd test all your solutions to see which works best. In the real world, you have limited time and resources—you must invest wisely.

For every solution you've built, score it on two factors:

1. Impact: How impactful is this solution in helping users overcome a specific challenge?
2. Cost: How much does it cost the business to offer this solution?

Challenge	Solution	Impact	Cost
Getting the event set up.	Free event page builder.	High	High
	List of the best event page designers.	Low	Low
	Blog post on what to include on your event page.	Medium	Low

The beauty of prioritizing based on Impact and Cost is that it vets solutions based on what's best for the business *and* the user.

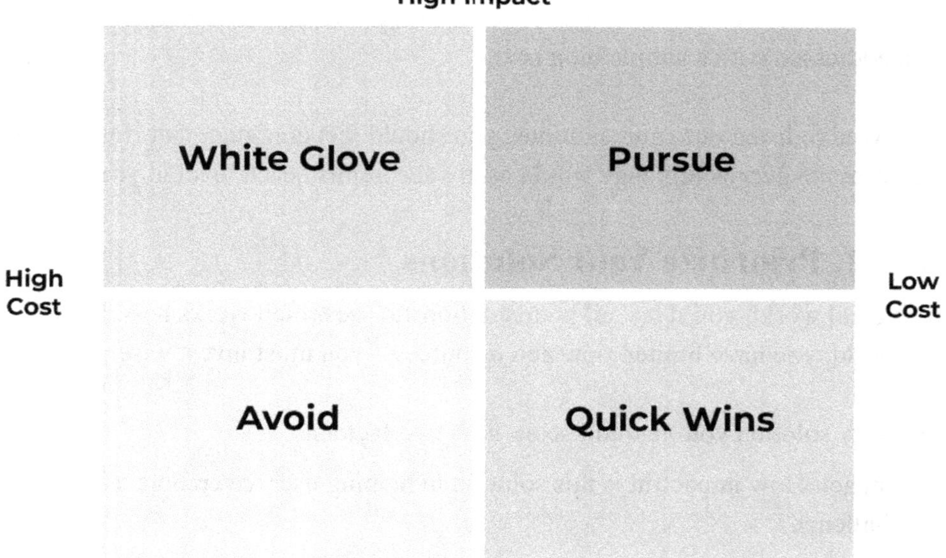

Here's how to think through prioritizing solutions:

- **Pursue:** If the solution is highly impactful to the user and low cost for the business to roll out and maintain, greenlight it.
- **White Glove:** Your solution is costly to roll out but it's highly impactful (e.g., free onboarding calls to every user). It won't scale, but it helps you learn more about users.
- **Quick Wins:** The solution isn't super impactful but it's easy to roll out (e.g., removing a bug that annoys users). It won't 10x the business but it's necessary.
- **Avoid:** If your solution isn't impactful and costs your business a lot, don't do it.

Make every potential solution fight for its life. Low-cost, high-impact solutions are wonderful but rare. Expect to make difficult decisions and kill most of the ones you identify.

Every team should be involved in identifying and creating solutions. The marketing team can create content about challenges. The sales team can create enablement resources for objection-related challenges. And so on.

Your Turn (To Fill Out)

Challenges	Solutions	Impact	Cost

Use the labels high, medium, and low to fill out your Impact and Cost columns.

Step 3: Shortlist Your Solutions

Shortlist everything so your team knows what needs to be built. You'll have clarity on what you're giving away for free and what you're moving behind a paywall.

List your top three challenges and the top three to five solutions for each level.

PromoTix Example:

Beginner Level	Intermediate Level	Advanced Level
Beginner Outcome: Publish an event page.	**Intermediate Outcome:** Sell more tickets with marketing tools.	**Advanced Outcome:** Save big on ticketing fees.
Challenges: • Getting the event set up. • Planning the event. • Selling the tickets.	**Challenges:** • Marketing the tickets. • Creating graphics for event promotion. • Booking talent or artists to boost ticket sales.	**Challenges:** • Ensuring the event has the necessary features and services for attendees, such as RFID ticketing. • Ambassador program that meets the needs of promoters. • Create Mobile App.
Solutions: • Free event page builder. • Payment processing options. • Embedded checkout.	**Solutions:** • Mailchimp marketing email integration. • Google, Facebook, and AdRoll tracking pixels.	**Solutions:** • RFID wristband fulfillment, access control, cashless payments & sponsor activations.

• Ticket inventory management. • Unlimited ticket types. • Guest list management. • Discount codes. • Sell merchandise. • Staff accounts with roles & permissions.	• Event photo generator.	• Branded mobile app & app CMS. • Ambassador tasks and rewards.

This is the foundation for your free model:

- You'll give away everything at the beginner level.
- The intermediate level is the first paid plan.
- The advanced level is where you'll charge the most and grow with your customers.

The first time you do this, focus on the beginner level.

If you have a usage-based product, list how many units of your product you'd need to give away for your user to see value (e.g., five free seats, three free boards, five free courses, etc.). Also, list how long users will need to roll out these solutions. It'll help you with the last phase.

Your Turn (To Fill Out):

Beginner Outcome:	
Challenges	**Solutions**

You've got a rough shape for your free model. Now, it's time to polish it so that users can easily understand what it is and how it works.

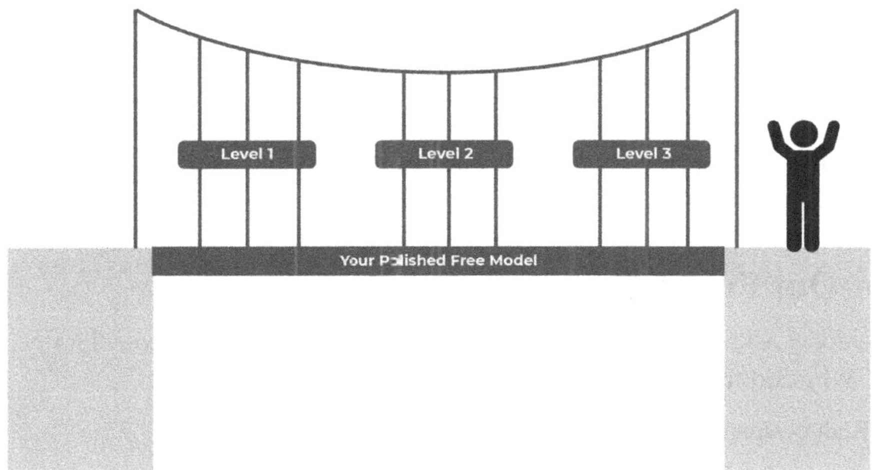

Phase 4: Polish – Identify What Free Model Works Best for Your Business

Many companies debate what to give away for free, yet only a few use a real strategy to support their opinions.

That won't be the case for your free model. You've already identified a meaningful win for your users, the big challenges, and solutions to overcome them. By the end of Phase 4, you'll have a clear one-pager that identifies what you're giving away for free and your overall product-led model.

Step 1: Discover the Six Main Product-Led Models

Before you pick a model, make sure you understand its advantages and disadvantages.

After learning about each model, try it on like a hat—what would it look like for your product?

Opt-in Free Trial

An opt-in free trial is among the most common product-led models.

Opt-in free trials are time-based and can be as long or short as needed for your user to experience the core value of the product. Users are attracted to this model because it doesn't require a credit card to sign up.

During your trial timeline, users can access most of the product's features to see whether they meet their needs. They'll likely stick around if they can get value within the allotted time (typically 7, 14, or 30 days).

Ask yourself whether users can find value in your product within the allotted timeframe; otherwise, the model won't work.

Opt-Out Free Trial

This model asks the user to provide credit card information to access the free trial. Why add friction?

1. Reduce spam signups.
2. Reduce the number of tire kickers.
3. Set a trigger for users to come back (e.g., an education product where most people don't have a natural trigger to consume content).
4. Avoid the cost of setting up a free trial for each user.
5. Avoid bogus email signups from recurring trial users if your product is used intermittently (e.g., an SEO tool like Ahrefs).
6. Work only with committed users if you're still manually onboarding users.

An opt-out free trial should be a last resort because it adds enormous friction and usually gets only a fraction of the sign ups of an opt-in free trial.

Your free-to-paid conversion rate will be higher than an opt-in free trial, but that's because most potential users didn't sign up in the first place. Overall, you typically make less money with an opt-out free trial. The higher free-to-paid conversion rate doesn't make up for the smaller number of trial starts.

Usage-Based Free Trial

Usage-based free trials are one of my favorite models. Instead of a time limit, you set a usage limit—exactly how much value you give away for free.

For example, I've been using Evernote for eight years on their forever-free plan. They gave me unlimited free notes to create, so I was happy. Evernote tried to upgrade me based on random features I didn't need (e.g., Do you want to design what your homepage on Evernote looks like?).

However, in early 2024, they changed to a usage-based free trial where I could create only 50 notes. I had created hundreds over the years, and I couldn't create more unless I upgraded. It took me 10 seconds to decide to upgrade. That's a usage-based model in action.

You'll see usage-based free trials at many world-class product-led businesses, such as Miro (three boards) and Vidyard (25 videos).

Usage-based free trials work because they allow users to access a limited amount of your product's full value rather than restricting features as you would with a freemium model. It's the difference between offering "a limited amount of all the value" versus "an unlimited amount of some of the value." This approach eliminates artificial time pressure and lets users experience the core benefits of your product at their own pace.

Freemium

Freemium is when you give away certain features—forever.

For instance, Canva has a generous freemium plan that allows you to create unlimited designs. However, there are limits to templates and features you can use. For example, you can't resize a template or use premium stock photos without upgrading.

Freemium works well when your product requires mastering a specific skill (e.g., design), and ideal users naturally move from solving beginner problems to more advanced ones, which, in turn, require access to more advanced features.

Freemium is the most powerful product-led model because it has the most compelling offer. Yet, it's also a high-risk model. Many ambitious entrepreneurs have tried and failed. Rob Walling, the previous CEO of Drip, offers a warning: "Freemium is like a Samurai sword: unless you're a master at using it, you can cut your arm off."

Another challenge with freemium for smaller companies is that it can attract a lot of non-paying users, who create distractions.

But maybe you don't need any of the above models. Maybe you need a new product.

New Product

I know what you're thinking. This isn't *really* a new product-led model. (You're right.)

But, going back to the Vidyard example, our biggest blocker was users not having a video to upload. Without it, they would almost never see the value of our solution.

A longer free trial or a different product-led model wouldn't solve the problem. So we designed a new product that made it super simple to record a video and made *that* tool free, which is still used by millions today.

Maybe you're not addressing the primary challenge that's holding users back from seeing value. In these situations, it typically makes sense to develop a new product to help users overcome their main challenge faster.

What if that's not an option? Sometimes, creating a sandbox is all you can do.

Sandbox

The sandbox model is a clickable product tour—the last resort.

It's not as exciting to play with dummy data and click around on a product. Nothing will ever replace seeing your data in a product. Yet the sandbox model can complement an existing model above.

This can often improve sign up rates. Users can quickly "take a tour" in your sandbox environment to see what the product is capable of and what success would look like. Then, they can sign up for your free model and see for themselves.

Typically, the sandbox model is reserved for companies with a long time to value and for which it's difficult to roll out the product.

So which model is right for your ideal user?

Step 2: Choose the Model That Best Allows Your Users to Experience the Value

Do you have to pick only one model or can you mix and match?

For instance, can you start with a premium free trial and then downgrade people to freemium? Yes, you absolutely can. But if it's your first time launching a product-led motion, don't be cute. Master the basics before considering a more complex hybrid model.

Choose one ideal model that helps users bridge the gap between where they are and their desired outcome. Then package it up as a one-pager.

Your Turn (To Fill In)

Product-Led Model (Check the box)	Reason
☐ Opt-In Free Trial ☐ Opt-Out Free Trial ☐ Usage-Based Free Trial ☐ Freemium ☐ New Product ☐ Sandbox	

Step 3: Put It All in a One-Pager

This is my favorite part.

You get to put the finishing touches and see how everything fits together. This one-page document outlines exactly what you're promising ideal users in your free plan.

Boil down what you're giving away for free into three to five bullet points.

PromoTix's Free Plan
Desired Outcome: Publish your event for free and start selling tickets.
Model: Freemium
Top challenges your ideal user will encounter: • Getting the event set up. • Planning the event. • Selling the tickets.
Solutions we're giving away: • Free event page builder. • Payment processing options. • Ticket inventory management. • Unlimited ticket types. • Staff accounts with roles & permissions.
(Optional) What's Included in future versions? • Event flyer generator • Ticket tier pricing model

Don't limit your offer to the behind-the-scenes functionality. For instance, instead of pitching "an event page to help users sell tickets," highlight that you're "giving the user everything they need to publish their first event." The first sounds underwhelming and tactical; the latter reads like tangible value.

There's also an optional section to shortlist more potential free components. When I go through this activity with teams, they often get excited about everything they could give away. But you can always add others later—and it's great to have a place to keep these ideas handy when re-assessing your free plan.

Voila! You've now built an intentional model that lets your product's true value shine in the free experience. To put everything together, we've created the One-Page Free Model Canvas.

One-Page Free Model Canvas

Company Name:

Designed by:

Date:

Beginner Outcome	
Top Challenges	Top Solutions
Model	Call-to-Action
(Optional) What to Include in the Future?	

Download a virtual copy here

Based on the book The Product-Led Playbook: How to Unlock Self-Serve Revenue and Dominate Your Market (With a Tiny Team)

ProductLed®

productled.com

Action Tool: One-Page Free Model Canvas

Download a virtual copy here.

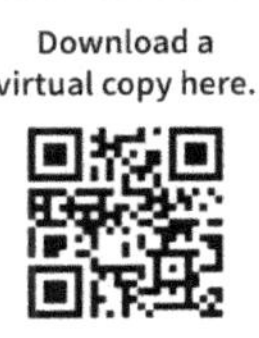

Head over to ProductLedPlaybook.com to put your free model into a one-page canvas you can share with the rest of your team.

Creating Your Intentional Free Model

Most times, your first free model won't work out. (Sorry, just setting expectations.) But you'll learn a ton from launching it. There's beauty in failing fast but learning faster. The only time you really fail is when you fail to learn from your mistakes.

So don't overanalyze your model to death. It's time to bring it to life.

Actionable Takeaways

- There is no single correct model. Instead of debating whether you should have a free trial vs. freemium model, focus on your user's desired outcome and their challenges, then arm them with everything they need to succeed. Align your model with those solutions.
- The best product-led models are Desirable for your users, Effective at showcasing value, Efficient for users to experience that value, and Polished.
- Your product's unique value needs to shine in your free experience. Don't hide your best stuff behind a paywall. Let it blow your free users away!
- Run the PCR test to identify out-of-the-box ideas for some of your toughest challenges.
- Your model needs to make a tangible difference in your user's life. Don't launch another mediocre model that leaves users exactly where they were. That's a wasted opportunity.

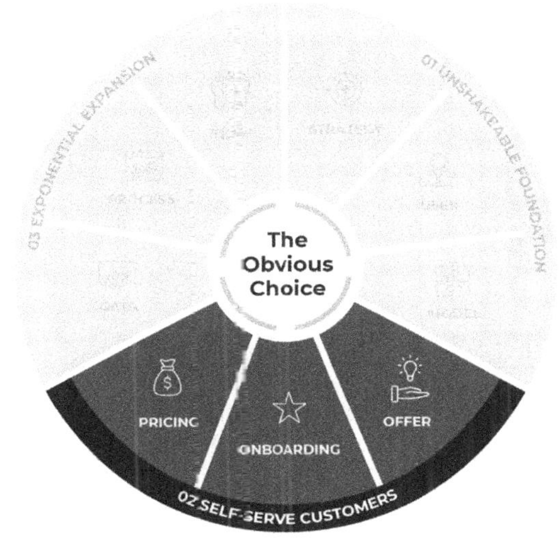

Stage 2

Unlock Self-Serve Customers

Go from “high-touch” to “zero-touch” customers.

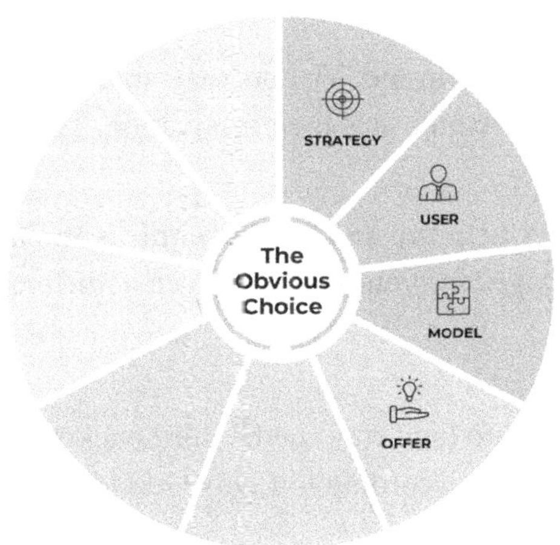

Irresistible Offer

How **irresistible** is your offer?

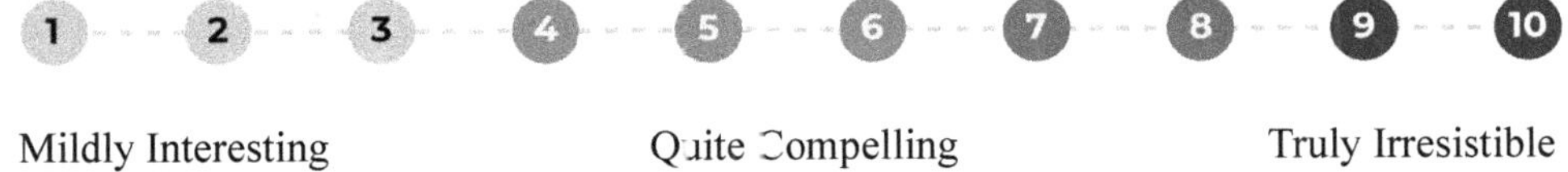

Mildly Interesting | Quite Compelling | Truly Irresistible

Rate yourself from 1 to 10.

You've just designed a free model that's genuinely going to help your users. Now, it's time to get as many people to try out that free offer—and make it so enticing that people would feel stupid to say no. It isn't easy.

Within seconds of landing on your homepage, users evaluate your business and your offer, placing you into one of three buckets:

1. **You can't help me.** Visitors will move on—even if you can solve their exact problem.
2. **You might be able to help me.** Visitors may sign up and check out your product, but the uncertainty saps their motivation. They often bail during onboarding.
3. **You can absolutely help me and I believe this is the best solution.** Users "get it" and are hungry for your solution, even at different stages of the user journey.

Why is it so hard to get into (and stay) in the third bucket? Because your offer needs to stand the f*ck out, according to Louis Grenier, author of *Stand the F*ck Out*.

Yet, want me to let you in on a little secret? If your strategy sucks, so will your offer. If your strategy is rock solid, your offer will be, too.

For instance, PromoTix is going up against Eventbrite, and they identified that they could win against Eventbrite with:

1. Lower prices.
2. Better marketing tools to help sell more tickets.

That's PromoTix's strategy for how to win. It leaned into those two big advantages in the homepage copy and increased signups by more than 40%—with the same amount of traffic!

It pays to have a clear strategy and differentiators. Hiring a magnificent copywriter alone won't cut it. Your visitors are smart. They can sniff out in a few seconds whether your solution is right for them. And if you make one of three major mistakes, they'll quickly conclude that it's not for them.

Mistake 1: Being Cute

You know what I'm talking about: Headlines that read, "We're the AI-enabled solution to your biggest challenges." So you do… what?

Your visitors will make a snap decision on whether you can help them or not. If you take forever to explain what your product does, how it helps them, and why they should choose you, they're going to find another solution. Your offer needs to be succinct. If your language is indirect, fluffy on benefits, or full of jargon, you're being too cute.

Mistake 2: No Enhancers

Chocolate ice cream is delicious on its own. Most people reading this would agree. Yet put peanut butter on it, and you've just taken that ice cream from a 7/10 to a 10/10 experience.

Without enhancers, you won't be irresistible (but another flavor of software will be).

Mistake 3: Lack of Structure

An offer page should flow like a story. You meet the villain (a big challenge), sign up for the product, and then beat the villain with your new powers.

Most offer pages lack structure or just ramble on about the greatness of the solution. A good book follows a structure, and your offer should, too.

We'll address all of these mistakes and more so you can significantly increase the number of users signing up for your product without increasing your traffic. Lucky for you, you don't have to be a copywriter. We've had many founders implement this process and unlock more conversions.

Introducing The 5-Star Offer Generator

This framework consists of three phases. By the end, you'll have a homepage that not only encourages visitors to sign up but gets them excited about using your product.

This phase builds on the foundation from the User and Model Components. I'll use PromoTix as an example throughout this component to highlight the importance of following the strategic order of the ProductLed System.

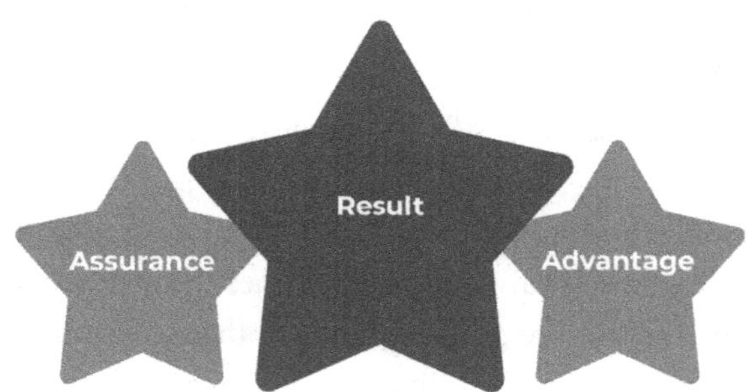

Phase 1: Core Offer

Defining your core offer answers why your product is awesome for users.

There are three pillars:

1. The Result
2. The Advantage
3. The Assurance

A great offer sits at the center of all three.

To establish these pillars, dig deep into your customer's psyche. Ask "why" at every stage to uncover the essence of their problem, along with the unique benefit your product provides. Otherwise, you're stuck at the surface level, blending in with the crowd.

Pillar 1: The Result

This is the tangible, measurable outcome your product delivers. It's not about vague benefits. What are you doing to help users save time or make money? Anything not directly attached to an outcome is not specific enough.

Take the case of a business with an email automation tool for WordPress. An ineffective approach would use vague terms such as "better," "faster," or a broad promise that it will "grow your business."

The better approach? Highlight specific, relevant benefits:

- "Designed for agencies using WordPress," eliminating the need to learn a new platform and saving time.
- "Flat-rate pricing," which translates to significant cost savings as an email list grows.

These points directly address user needs and position the product in a compelling way.

To get started on your offer, revisit how you defined the endgame for your ideal users (from the User Component).

PromoTix User Endgame
Hosting consistently profitable, sold-out events with happy attendees

Next, define the top three results successful users will notice. Ideally, these are measurable. Often, they break down into three groups:

1. A very tangible result that all users will see (e.g., self-serve revenue increases).
2. An intangible outcome (e.g., more peace of mind).
3. An improvement (e.g., revenue-per-employee improves).

If you filled out the top three outcomes from the User Component, you might be able to use those here as well.

User Endgame: Hosting consistently profitable, sold-out events with happy attendees
Results
Help event organizers be more profitable.
Drive more sales with marketing tools.
Start selling quickly by publishing your event.

Your Turn (To Fill In)

User Endgame:	
Results	

Once you've identified the top three results, explain why your product is better.

Pillar 2: The Advantage

How is your product significantly better than other options on the market?

Most founders can't answer this question—so their potential customers can't either. A marginally better product won't convince potential customers to switch.

Claims like "we're easier to use" or "our platform is faster" won't cut it. Dig deeper. Why is your product five or 10x better than the competition?

- Zoom has a great audio filter that blocks all background noise and allows users to make calls from bustling coffee shops.
- Canva is far easier to use than Adobe Photoshop.
- PromoTix is up to 40% cheaper than alternatives like Eventbrite.

Write down your product's advantages. Think holistically. Why is your approach the best?

User Endgame: Hosting consistently profitable, sold-out events with happy attendees
Advantages
Low ticketing fees.
Start selling in under five minutes.
Start selling quickly by publishing your event.

Next, run them through the "Why does it matter?" test.

Let's say your platform has a better user experience—why does this matter? If all solutions in your space are extremely hard to use, this could be a major benefit. If not, then it's not the advantage to lead with.

If you're still struggling, go back to your "how to win" strategy. Your moats should reinforce your advantages.

For instance, if your how-to-win moats are:

- A differentiated approach.
- A unique pricing model.
- Great user experience.

Call out those specific advantages! It's great if your main advantages closely align with your strategy—it shows that what you're putting into the market aligns with your strategy.

Your Turn (To Fill In)

User Endgame:	
Advantages	

It pays to have clear advantages, but you also need to identify why some visitors still don't sign up.

Pillar 3: The Assurance

If potential customers believe switching to your product is a risk, they won't make the leap—regardless of your offer. Addressing fears and uncertainties directly can make all the difference.

For example, for Kloudle, a cloud security platform, visitors might want to know:

- Will setup be difficult?
- What cloud providers do you support?
- What compliance and security measures are in place?

Address those fears and explain in concrete terms why they're unfounded. Be specific about why there's no risk. In this example, this company could detail the average number of minutes it takes to set up based on past customer experiences. Here are common objections and assurances for SaaS companies.

Common Objections	Common Assurances
ROI	Money-Back Guarantee: A promise to refund the purchase if the customer is not satisfied within a certain timeframe.
	Price Match Guarantee: A promise to match a lower price found elsewhere for the same product.
	Satisfaction Guarantee: An assurance that the customer will be satisfied with the product or service, often backed by a refund or exchange policy.
Setup & Training	Onboarding and Training: Offering free or discounted onboarding and training services to ensure the customer can use the software effectively.
Support	Customer Support Guarantee: Guaranteeing access to dedicated customer support, often with specific response and resolution times.
Collaboration	Free Trials: Allowing customers to use the product or service for a limited time before committing to a purchase.
Security	Social Proof: Showcasing awards and recommendations from reputable companies to boost your credibility.

Identify your top three objections and address those risks in concrete terms. Explain why those fears are unfounded. Quantify everything. Offer assurance.

Here's what this looks like for PromoTix.

Objection	Assurance
Upfront cost to set up the event.	No credit card is required to start.
Doesn't work for both big and small events.	Complete attendee management.
I won't be able to sell many tickets.	Sell 22% more tickets with our marketing tools.

Your Turn (To Fill In)

Objection	Assurance

Combining It All

All three pillars are critical:

- If a company communicates only the results and assurances, why should you use that solution?
- If a company communicates its results and advantages, what are the risks of signing up?
- If a company communicates the assurances and the advantages, what are the results?

Now that you have an irresistible offer, it's time to enhance it.

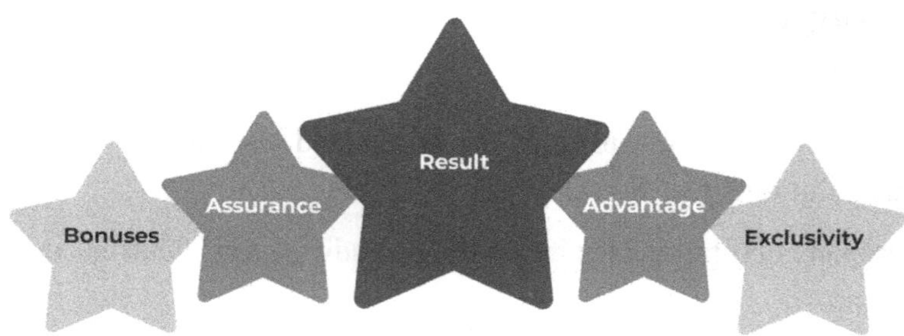

Phase 2: Enhancers

Start with a solid core offer. Let enhancers take that offer from a 7/10 to a 10/10. This can mean up to 15% more conversions.

Deciding what these enhancers are doesn't take long, but the impact is almost immediate. You have two main options: exclusivity and bonuses.

Exclusivity

Exclusivity is driven by scarcity and urgency.

Can you handle only a limited number of customers each month? Do you want to cap your beta program to, say, 100 spots? Do you want to invite only a few people to test out your new free motion?

Every business has something that'll break if you add too many customers to it. Artificial scarcity doesn't work, but consider whether you can add authentic scarcity to the mix.

Scarcity is one reason to sign up now. Urgency is another. Your biggest competitor isn't your competitor. It's people who continue doing the same thing the same way.

Forms of urgency include:

1. A limited-time offer.
2. Exploding opportunity. (e.g., PLG is hot. If you don't do it, a competitor will.)
3. Cohort-based urgency. (e.g., You have a firm deadline on when you can no longer accept enrollments.)
4. Bonus-based urgency. (e.g., A free gift disappears after a certain period of time.)

Let's dig into bonuses a bit more.

Bonuses

A good bonus excites potential users. But most bonuses are random: "Open a new bank account and get a free toaster!"

Good bonuses tie back to your User and Model Components. They address challenges that haven't been addressed yet. For instance, if your software is a user onboarding solution, users may struggle to understand the principles of how to onboard their users effectively.

So what do you offer? Give users a free user onboarding course. Typically, this is valued at $999, but if they sign up this month, they'll get it for free. That's a compelling offer.

Other types of bonuses include:

- Free gifts
- Free resources (assessments, training)
- 1:1 expert support
- Free audits

ProductLed client Keap.com noticed that many customers churned in the first few months because small business owners rarely automate important processes—a core differentiator. So, they gave away a free audit to help business owners identify one crucial process to automate, then set it up for them. This one bonus skyrocketed Keap's retention.

What enhancers can you offer?

You don't have to use every enhancer. Identify three to help assemble your offer. Put everything in the Irresistible Offer Canvas for reference and share with your team.

Once you've built out your irresistible offer, you're ready to get more signups with a high-converting homepage.

Company Name:

Designed by:

Date:

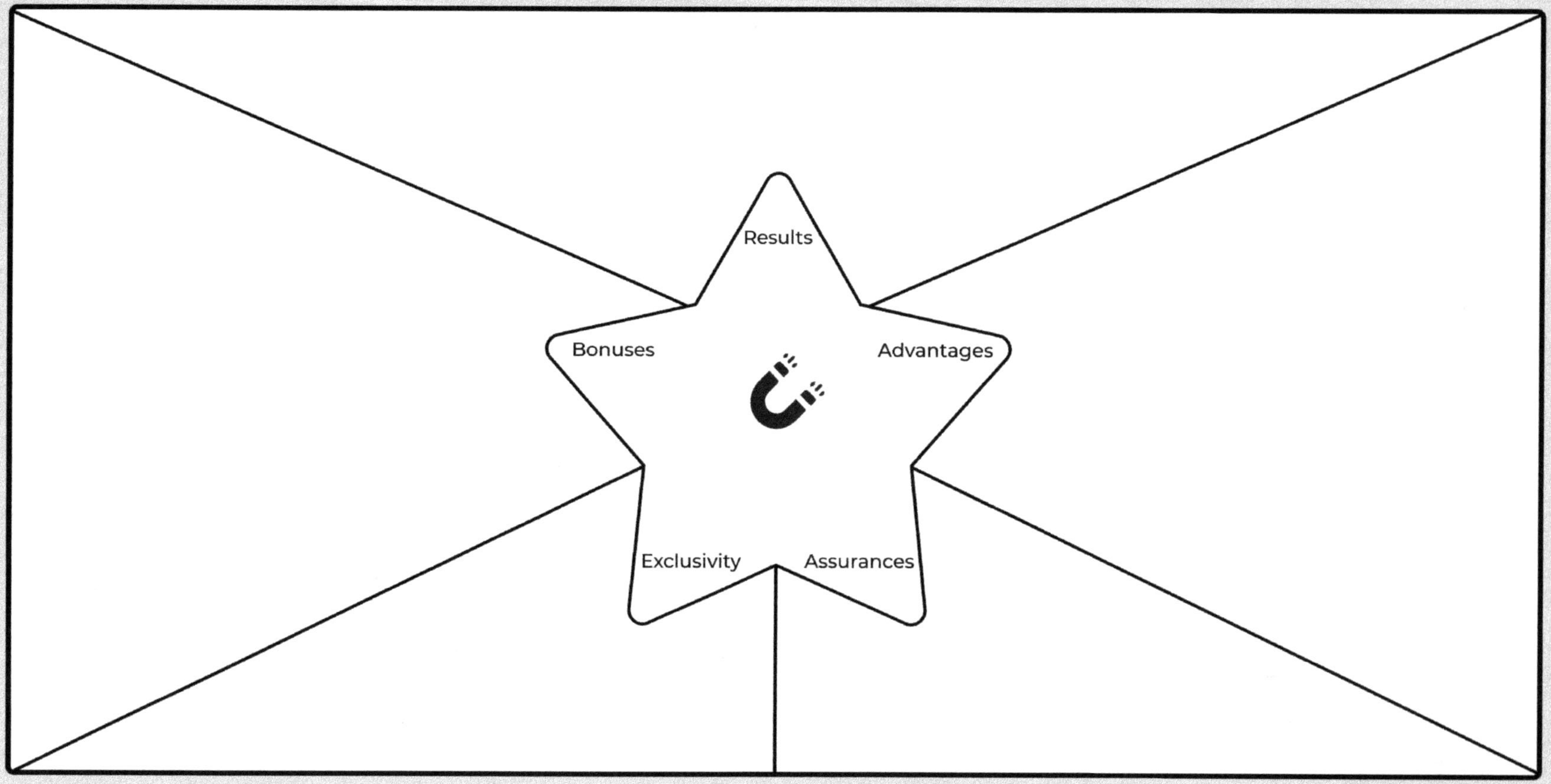

Results

Bonuses

Advantages

Exclusivity

Assurances

Based on the book The Product-Led Playbook: How to Unlock Self-Serve Revenue and Dominate Your Market (With a Tiny Team)

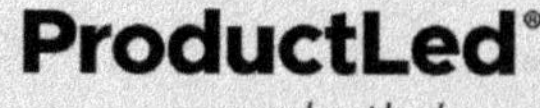

🎁 Action Tool: Irresistible Offer Canvas

Grab our free Irresistible Offer Canvas at ProductLedPlaybook.com to follow along with this activity.

Download a virtual copy here.

Phase 3: Assemble Your Offer

Your offer page needs five sections:

1. A **Hero Section** gets your attention by clearly communicating the main value proposition—what you'll get from the product.
2. A **Problem Section** clearly communicates the main problem your product solves and builds interest around the potential solution.
3. A **Solution Section** explicitly answers the "How does it work?" question that so many users want to know before signing up.
4. A **Risk Reversal Section** addresses the main reasons that might prevent someone from signing up.
5. A **Call-to-Action Section** asks the user to sign up and gives compelling reasons to support why they need to take action.

Don't overcomplicate your homepage—these five are all you need. It's tempting to delegate this step to a copywriter but complete the first draft yourself. Messaging matters. You're the expert.

Let's take a look at PromoTix's changes—and the resulting impact.

Hero Section

Your Hero Section contains the first words users see and is arguably the most important part of your homepage. It's the first impression of what you do as a business, and in seconds, users will decide whether they should continue scrolling through—or ditch—your site.

There are five pieces:

1. A tagline that communicates the result you offer.
2. Sub-copy that reinforces what you do as a business and prompts users to start.
3. A call-to-action (CTA) that's a simple prompt to take the first step to sign up.
4. A visual aid is optional but can quickly communicate what your product does in ways that words can't.
5. Social proof assures users that you're a reputable business.

Since you've already done the hard work of filling out your Irresistible Offer Canvas, completing the Hero section is a lot easier. You'll notice that your offer is a lot more specific and speaks directly to your ideal users.

To show you the massive impact this can have, look at the changes PromoTix made to its Hero Section.

	Old Copy	New Copy
Value Prop	Built for event creators.	Sell more tickets without insanely high ticketing fees.
Subtitle	Low ticketing fees. Powerful marketing. Live streaming. We make events more profitable.	Finally, there's a way to market and sell more tickets without needing a ton of other marketing tools and without high ticket service fees. Get your event up and selling in under 5 minutes.
CTA	Sign Up	Ticket My Event
Visual	A picture of an event.	A picture of a big crowd at an event.
Social Proof	Some customer logos.	Awards from Capterra, SourceForge & Slashdot.

Your Turn (To Fill In)

Value Prop	
Subtitle	
CTA	
Visuals	
Social Proof	

Once you've grabbed the attention of your user, educate them on their core problem.

Problem Section

A good Problem Section quickly points out why the current approach is not the best path forward.

Your Problem Section might point out problems:

- With other tools.
- With current (non-SaaS) solutions.
- The broader, underlying problem.

What obstacle blocks users from seeing value? Wes Kao, co-founder of Maven, refers to this as your "spiky point of view." It should be a tad controversial—not over the top, but not something everyone agrees with. If you've identified the underlying reason why you're better as a business, your spiky point of view plays into it.

For instance, at ProductLed, what makes us better is our holistic approach to product-led growth. So when our problem statement is "Product-led growth is more than a free trial," it reflects our belief that a free trial is just one piece of the puzzle.

Don't shy away from confrontation. PromoTix embraced it. The Department of Justice is suing its competitors for high ticketing fees[10] (among other things), something important for them to highlight. Their problem statement is, "Ticketmaster, eTix, Eventbrite, and others have service fees ranging from 20 to 40%, and the fees are climbing…"

If your users don't have comparable solutions, ask: What should scare them if they don't use your product?

	Old Copy	New Copy
Spiky Point of View	Before we built PromoTix, our executive team threw and organized events, festivals, concerts, and owned venues. We saw what was broken with traditional ticketing that didn't meet our needs and created PromoTix.	Ticketmaster, eTix, Eventbrite, and others have service fees ranging from 20 to 40%, and the fees are climbing…
Top Challenges	You're not equipped with the marketing tools you need to drive ticket sales.	You're losing a significant chunk of your revenue to excessive fees.
Agreeable Viewpoint	Sell more tickets with PromoTix.	Make more with PromoTix.

If you're struggling to identify the core problem, go back to the problem statement from the Strategy Component. It should overlap. Also, your top challenges should overlap with challenges identified in the Model Component for the free model.

Intrigue your ideal user with a spiky point of view, list some of the top challenges holding them back, and leave them aligned with your perspective. (Note: This won't mean *everyone* is aligned. You want to turn away non-ideal users.)

Your Turn (To Fill In)

Spiky Point of View	
Top Challenges	
Agreeable Viewpoint	

Unlike the Hero Section, which is clear-cut, your Problem Section is flexible.

To see if you're on the right path, write your Problem Section out as a LinkedIn post and see if it strikes a chord. If it falls flat, you don't have a spiky point of view. If it drives a lot of engagement, you're onto something.

Solution Section

A good Solution Section answers the "How does it work?" question. A great Solution Section reinforces the underlying result and outlines how users can achieve it.

Most companies overcomplicate it, listing all the required steps. Ideally, you have no more than five. (They don't have to be sequential.)

	Old Copy	New Copy
Headline	Make more with PromoTix.	Here's how to sell more tickets and make 10 to 20% more revenue. Get your event up and running, in less than five minutes.
Why is your solution the best?	Stop letting your current ticketing provider take advantage of you and your attendees, and stop leaving money on the table. You deserve more from your ticketing company.	Festivals, concerts, venues, shows, and other event creators increase bottom-line profits by an average of 27% with PromoTix.
Steps	1. Sign up for PromoTix. 2. Add revenue with live streaming. 3. Sell more with powerful marketing features.	1. Take 10 to 20% of your attendee revenue back. 2. Publish your event in under five minutes. 3. Use our marketing tools to sell up to 22% more tickets.

A compelling Solution Section makes users feel like they can achieve the result by reading the copy alone. Give users a taste of what solving this problem feels like.

Your Turn (To Fill In)

Headline	
Why is your solution the best?	
Steps	

You'll still have some skeptical users. Let's fix that.

Risk Reversal Section

Visitors understand your offer, what's unique about it, and how it works for them. Yet, out of every 100 visitors, only a few will take action. Why?

Someone on your team probably has a hunch. Start listing every reason your team has heard about why a potential customer didn't sign up. You'll spot patterns.

For many software companies, an objection will look something like:

- What is my ROI?
- What is the setup time?
- Does it work with other tools?

Confront these objections head-on with social proof. When visitors spot a familiar logo or testimonial from a respected brand, they instantly feel a wave of trust.

Deploy social proof alongside every section, including right below the above-the-fold section. Include it in each step of your Solution Section to expand on how easy it was, how much time was saved, or how big the result was.

Expand it into a before-and-after story from a customer to reinforce the difference between what it was like before your solution and what it's like now.

Objections	Risk Reversal
What is my ROI?	Get 10 to 20% of your revenue back.
How long does it take to set up?	Get your event up and selling in under 5 minutes.
Will I be able to sell enough tickets?	Sell up to 22% more tickets with powerful marketing tools.

You can also reverse risk using:

- Guarantees.
- Endorsements from influential people in your space.
- User reviews and ratings (G2, Trustpilot, etc).
- Client logos that can quickly communicate you've worked with other credible brands.
- Media coverage.
- Customer or user count.
- Showcasing a demo version of your product they can easily explore before signing up.
- Certifications/Third-party accreditations.

Your Turn (To Fill In)

Objections	Risk Reversal

You've reduced the risks; now make it a no-brainer to sign up.

Call-to-Action Section

A good call-to-action (CTA) asks the user to sign up and gives compelling reasons to do so.

Don't introduce new content or insights. Lean into the top reason why someone should sign up, why your solution is better, and why it's less risky—a proven formula for great results.

Why sign up now?	Take home up to 20% more profit starting today.
What can they do once they sign up?	Publish your event for free.
Is it risk-free?	No credit card is required.
What's the next step?	Ticket your event.

Your Turn (To Fill In)

Why sign up now?	
What can they do once they sign up?	
Is it risk-free?	
What's the next step?	

At this point, you've built the crux of your irresistible offer. You may need to refine this offer further or send it to design and marketing teams. Set an aggressive deadline to ship this page. Even if it doesn't feel "perfect," launch.

Action Tool: High-Converting Homepage Template

Grab our free homepage template at ProductLedPlaybook.com to follow along with this activity.

Download a virtual copy here.

Once it's live, you can edit it over time. Too often, companies spend months refining internally when they could be getting real user feedback.

PromoTix saw great results by A/B testing their new homepage first, which minimized the risk. After a week, signups increased by 40% on the new page, giving them the confidence to roll it out to 100%.

You've crafted an offer. You've communicated it. Now, deliver on it.

Actionable Takeaways

- A good strategy is a prerequisite to a good offer. If your offer is missing teeth, odds are it's because you have a mediocre strategy.
- Your core offer cuts through the noise and simplifies your product. You must be clear on what the main results are that your product helps users achieve, the main advantages to using your solution, and the top assurances that you can offer to de-risk signing up for your solution.
- Enhancers can take a 7/10 offer to a 10/10 offer. They won't make an irresistible offer on their own, but they can easily squeeze out an additional 5 to 15% more signups if used properly. Use scarcity, urgency and bonuses to make it a no-brainer for anyone to sign up.
- A good structure is imperative to allowing users to quickly understand what your product is all about. Start with a compelling Hero section, then build interest with your Problem Section, break down your Solution Section, reduce the risk of signing up, and end with a compelling CTA.

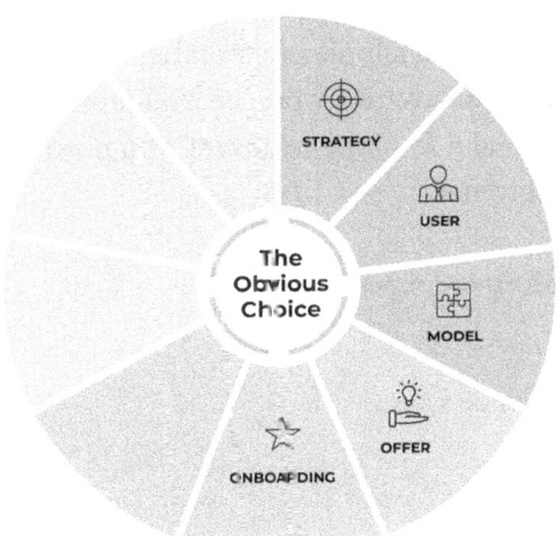

Frictionless Onboarding

How **easy** is it to sign up and get to value in your product?

Difficult Smooth Effortless

Rate yourself from 1 to 10.

Forty to 60% of users who sign up for your product never return. It's a bloodbath. Most users who sign up genuinely want to experience your product's value, but challenges get in their way.

Take Snappa. They required every new signup to activate their email address before logging into the product—27% of signups never took that step. They never even saw the product.

I pretend that every user says a simple prayer after signing up: "Please make this easy!" It's up to us to answer their prayer. You promised something. They had faith. To turn them into true believers, you need to deliver—ideally, overdeliver—on your promise.

You must create an effortless experience:

1. Effortless to sign up.
2. Effortless to experience value.
3. Effortless to upgrade.

How do you avoid the Snappa scenario and make that happen?

Deploy the Bowling Alley Framework

I've successfully used the Bowling Alley Framework to help brands make millions—without spending a dime more on marketing. Whatever industry you're in, this system can help you craft an effortless experience that turns users into customers.

By simplifying the path for users to experience the value of your product, you skyrocket their odds of upgrading. In fact, this is how Snappa grew its MRR by 20% in one week, simply by deploying this framework.[11]

If you haven't played 10-pin bowling before, here's how it works. Ten pins stand in a triangular array 60 feet away. Between you and the pins, there's an oiled wooden lane 41.5 inches wide. You have a ball a little less than 9 inches in diameter that weighs up to 16 pounds. Your goal is to roll your ball down the lane and knock down as many pins as you can.

Here's the bad news: There are gutters on the left and right edges of the lane. If your ball falls into the gutter, you won't knock down any pins or get any points.

If you're new to 10-pin bowling, it's frustrating when your ball goes into the gutter. To fix this, Phil Kinzer invented the concept of "bumper bowling," in which a bumper keeps balls from going into the gutters. Avoiding the gutters virtually guarantees that you'll knock down pins.

You can win more customers by adding bumpers to your product experience.

When users get sidetracked or leave the product, bump them back in the right direction. Guide users to the part of the product that matters most. You'll keep users from trailing off and increase the number of those who return to the product.

With the Bowling Alley Framework, even a newbie can get a strike. This is crucial. As you eliminate challenges from your users' experience, your total addressable market expands—allowing more people to experience the value of your product.

By the end of this component, you'll know how to create an effortless onboarding experience. Start by defining your straight line.

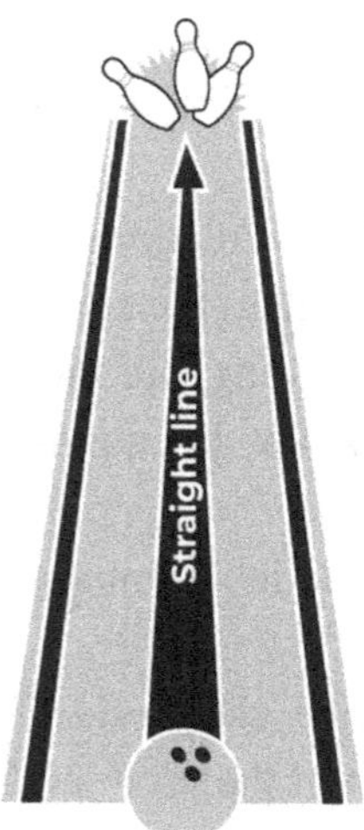

Phase 1: Build Your Straight Line

A straight line is the shortest distance from Point A to Point B.

The problem, however, is that most users never make it to Point B, where they experience the value of your product. Why? Most often, we don't know the desired outcome people are looking for—the reason they signed up.

Take Canva. You can use the product to create posters, cards, presentations, you name it. Given the incredible number of use cases, Canva created a web page that shows exactly how to create a poster. You simply click the CTA to create a poster, and within seconds, you're editing a poster in the product.

By understanding the problems people are trying to solve (e.g., how to make a poster) and customizing the onboarding experience to help users solve them, Canva slashed its time-to-value in half. It created a straight line. You should, too.

Step 1: Map Out the Fast Path

In my experience, 50% of required user onboarding steps are rubbish. (Yes, yours, too.) Many are required steps first-time users don't need to complete right away. Some don't need to be there at all.

When you first build out your straight line, map out a path to accomplishing a First Strike in your user journey—everything from Visit to First Strike is fair game. The second time you go through this activity, complete the straight line to the KUI. The third time, to the Upgrade step.

Why not map out the full experience right away? You typically lose 40 to 60% of your users during the First Strike step of your user journey, so optimizing this section will have the biggest impact.

Let's pretend you're an established ecommerce business with multiple Amazon and eBay stores. Every day, you spend three hours manually logging into each account to respond to customer messages. The more eBay and Amazon accounts you have, the more logging in and out you need to do.

After some research, you find our ProductLed client, ChannelReply, which has a product that allows you to forward all of your Amazon and eBay messages to a help-desk solution of your choice (e.g., Zendesk).

Once you sign up for ChannelReply's free trial, you integrate your Amazon and eBay accounts with the one help-desk solution. Once that's complete, you see messages pop up in your help-desk solution from eBay and Amazon—it's a miracle! This is when you decide to upgrade. The product delivered on its promise.

Naturally, ChannelReply wants everyone to get to this point in their user journey, but integrating a help desk with Amazon and eBay takes more than 50 steps. To develop a straight line, they need to reduce the number of steps.

To map out the ideal path, document every step from the second someone lands on your homepage until they hit the First Strike. Even small steps like clicking an "OK" button count.

You can go one step further and take a screenshot of every step. This will help you visualize every step users take to reach value.

After that, it's time to learn more about who's signing up.

Step 2: Add Your Profiling Questions

Add *more* steps? You just told me to kill all these steps! Hear me out.

Profiling questions are added right after a user signs up for your product. They help you quickly identify an ideal user and personalize the user journey so you can deliver value more quickly. While it adds friction, users will thank you if you use that information to personalize their dashboard, settings, and features.

Ask as few questions as possible. Users haven't seen the value of your product, so you need to balance friction with value.

For example, ChannelReply might ask users two questions at signup:

1. Where are you selling online? (e.g., Walmart, Amazon, eBay)
2. What help desk solution do you use? (e.g., HelpScout, Zendesk, Freshdesk)

These questions allow them to show the steps necessary to integrate specific marketplaces with their solution. If someone isn't selling on one of the platforms they support or doesn't use a compatible help desk solution, they're not an ideal user.

When deciding on your profiling questions, ask:

1. What question(s) could I ask to quickly identify if this is an ideal user or not?
2. What question(s) could I ask that would allow me to catapult users to value quickly?

Here's an example from Monday.com:

1. How do you want to use Monday.com?
    a. **For my team**
    b. For personal use
    c. For school

2. What best describes your current role?
    a. **Business owner**
    b. Team leader

   c. Team member
   d. Freelancer
   e. Director
   f. C-level/VP

3. What's the size of your current company?
   a. 1-10
   b. 11-49
   c. **50-199**
   d. 200-499
   e. 500+

4. What would you like to manage first?
   a. Sales and CRM
   b. Design and creative
   c. Education
   d. **Product management**

5. Select what you'd like to focus on first
   a. **Roadmap planning**
   b. Task management
   c. Project management

Within five questions, Monday.com knows if I'm an ideal user. This helps determine the level of support they should give me. It also gives them the opportunity to drop me into the product that would help me the quickest—in this case, roadmap planning templates.

As you'll learn in the Data Component, identifying an ideal user will ensure you're driving the right users to sign up.

Your Turn (To Fill In)

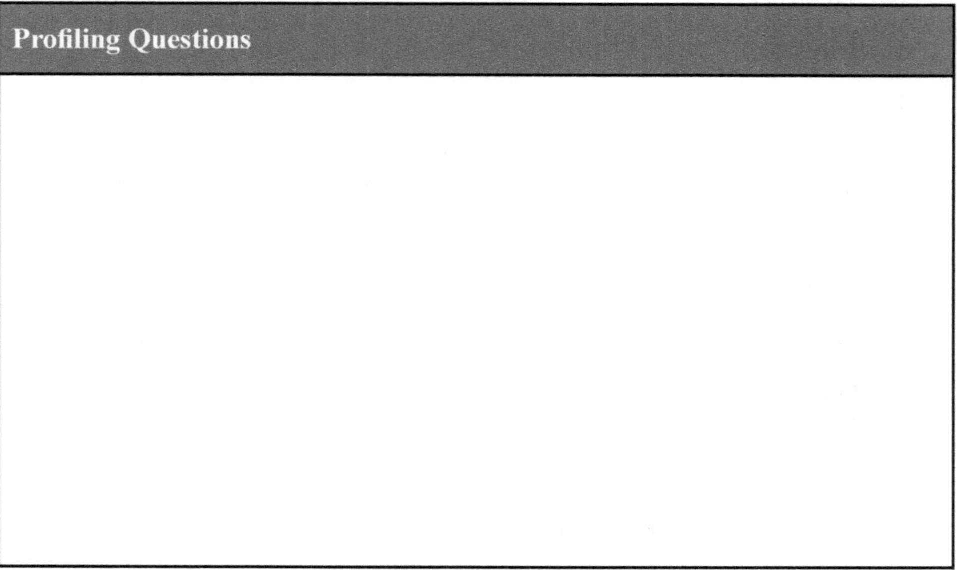

Once you've added profiling questions, it's time to label each step.

Step 3: Label Each Step

Now that you've mapped every step it takes for users to reach their desired outcome, label each with green, yellow, or red:

- Green is absolutely necessary (e.g., uploading a piece of JavaScript to your website or asking for an email address to set up an account).
- Yellow is for advanced features that can be introduced later (e.g., setting up a custom signature for your email address, or running split tests on video thumbnails).
- Red can be removed completely (e.g., changing the color of your profile picture or asking for someone's nickname when setting up their account).

Yellow is the hardest to label. Typically, it's a necessary step. But it's not needed *at that moment.* You can delay that step until later. Removing red steps and delaying yellow steps straightens the line that speeds users to success.

For ChannelReply, these might be the first three steps for account integration:

1. Integrate your Amazon account.
2. Set up your custom signature.
3. Share your nickname.

Integrating your Amazon account is necessary, so you'll label it green. Do you need a custom signature to see incoming messages from Amazon? No. Setting your custom signature is an advanced step. Once you see the product's value, it'll make sense. For now, label this step yellow. Lastly, sharing your nickname is totally unnecessary. Hence, you'll label this step red and remove it altogether.

Now you have all the components to create your straight line.

Step 4: Define Your Straight Line

Growing up in Hamilton, Canada, I took a bus to get to my downtown school. It took between one and two hours. Why the variance? The parade of stoplights. The bus was constantly starting, stopping, and idling.

To reduce the idling of cars and speed up traffic, the City of Hamilton introduced a green light sequence for Main Street, the busiest road in the city—and the main road my bus traveled along. If you hit one green light, you kept hitting green lights until you turned off Main Street.

This one innovation helped me get to school 25% faster.

This is how you want your straight line to feel for users: an unbroken string of green lights.

Once you've already broken down each step between signup and the First Strike, meet with your team to discuss all the steps you can potentially remove. Cut out as many red and yellow lights as possible. If you want a lively discussion, include people from product, engineering, marketing, and sales.

Keep only essential, green steps.

Step	Color
Where are you selling online?	Green
What help desk solution do you use?	Green
Integrate your Amazon account.	Green

That is the straight line to experiencing value in your product.

One of the reasons I love building a straight line is because every step needs to fight for its life. By the end, you'll learn that users simply need to complete steps X, Y, and Z for you to deliver your product's core value.

Companies consistently kill 30 to 40% of steps, delay another 20% of steps, and thrive with a fraction of the steps left in their straight line.

A straight-line onboarding experience makes it 2 to 3X easier for users to experience the core value of your product.

Even if you create the best possible straight-line experience, users still find a way to get stuck in the gutters (and never return to your product). You can solve this by installing two types of bumpers: product and conversational.

Phase 2: Product Bumpers

Product bumpers help users adopt the product within the application itself. If you've clicked on tooltips or checklists when you first signed up for a product, you've experienced product bumpers first-hand.

Product bumpers—arguably the most important bumper—help users experience meaningful value in the product. If you help users accomplish something meaningful, they'll come back.

Here are the main product bumpers:

Welcome Messages: Welcome messages greet new users and make them feel invited. Use them as an opportunity to say hello and restate your value proposition to increase motivation. These also set expectations for what users will experience with your product.

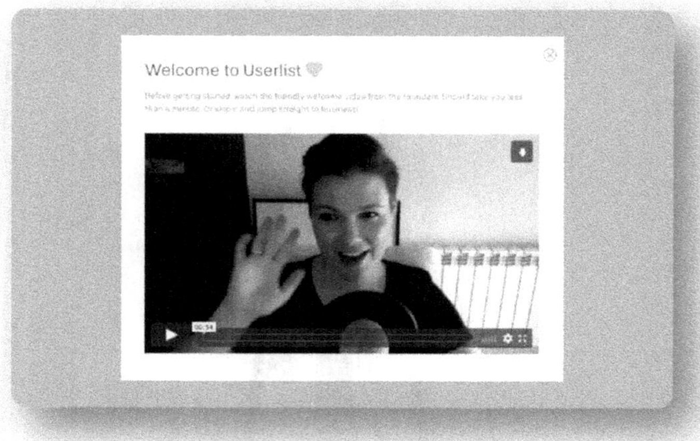

Product Tours: These eliminate distractions and give users only a few important options. If you have a multi-product business, a product tour at the beginning of your onboarding can be a game-changer. You catapult users into the areas of the product they care most about.

If you have a simple consumer application, you might be able to get away without a product tour. However, a product tour is a must for a complex product with features that accomplish different tasks.

I love using product tours to ask profiling questions right after someone signs up. Once users answer those questions, you can launch them into the part of the product they care most about.

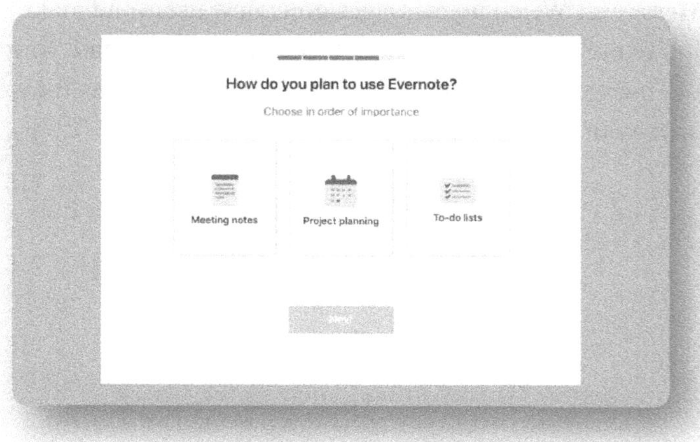

Progress Bars: Progress bars indicate how far a user has come and how far they need to go. You're setting an expectation for how many steps are ahead to reassure them that onboarding won't take long and that they're only a few steps from completion.

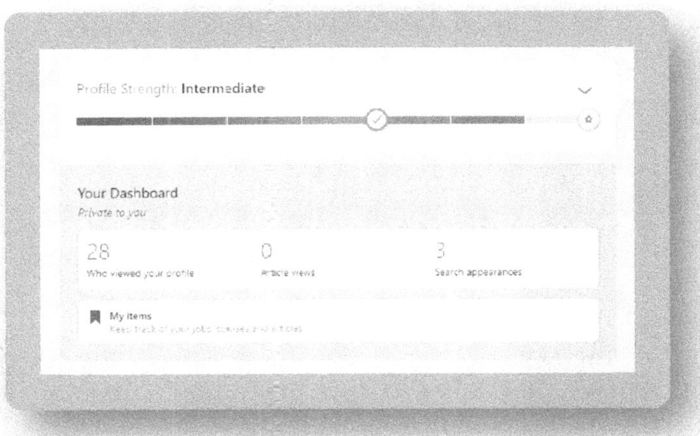

Checklists: Checklists break down big tasks into bite-sized ones. In addition to giving users an overview of how to set up their accounts, checklists simultaneously increase user motivation because users know how many steps it takes. Maximize their value by partially filling them out before the user sees them.

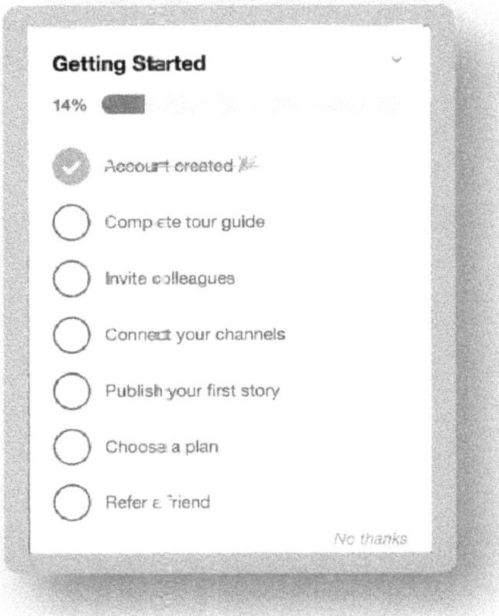

Onboarding Tooltips: These help users learn how to use a product. They can reduce the burden on support and scale usability. They offer helpful tips to new users and show experienced users new areas of the product.

Don't drown users in a sea of tooltips. Keep it simple—guide them through the straight-line onboarding steps.

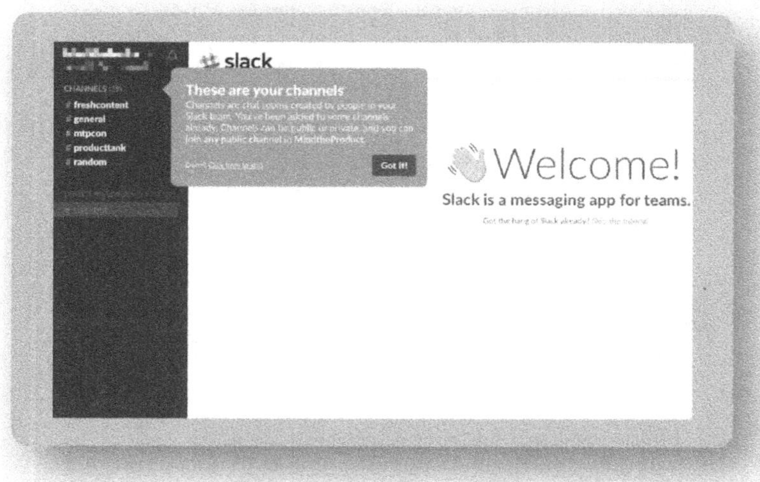

Empty States: Empty states are useful when a user first lands on a product's dashboard. Empty states should prompt users to take action that leads them closer to experiencing meaningful value.

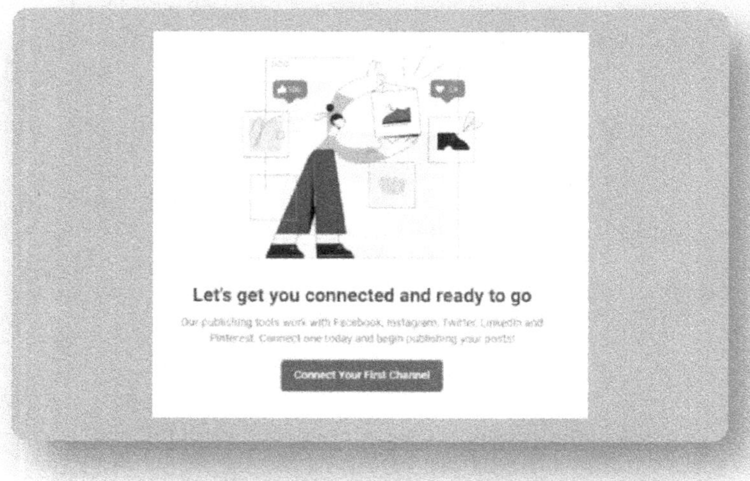

Do you *have* to use empty states, onboarding tooltips, checklists, and product tours? Absolutely not. Use product bumpers only when there's a need (i.e. when users are dropping off—more on that in the Data Component).

Each bumper is an opportunity to guide users toward the outcome that motivated their signup. Once you've installed your product bumpers, it's not uncommon to double the number of users who reach value and upgrade. Coincidence? I think not.

Let's explore how to pair product bumpers with conversational ones.

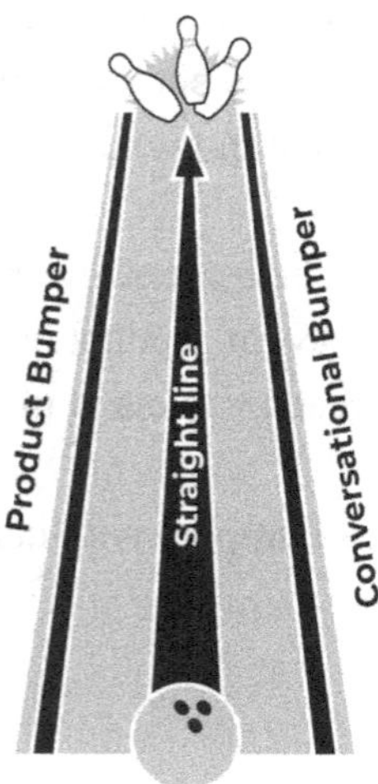

Phase 3: Conversational Bumpers

If someone signs up for your product but never sets foot in it, the best product bumpers won't help you. Conversational bumpers will.

Conversational bumpers educate users. They bring users back to the application and encourage them to upgrade their accounts. Whether you're using email, push notifications, explainer videos, direct mail, or even SMS, any communication medium can be a bumper.

Here are four reasons to use conversational bumpers:

1. Educate users.
2. Meet users where they are and pull them back into your product.
3. Increase motivation to use and buy your product.
4. Assist users in any way your product can't.

Imagine I signed up for your software but didn't complete the key setup stage in the onboarding process. How could you support me?

- You could send an email asking if I need help setting up the product.
- You could send me an automated email with instructions on how to complete the setup stage quickly.
- You could text me a quick reminder to complete the setup stage.
- You could offer a free onboarding call to walk me through the process.

You can do so many things with conversational bumpers, which allow companies to smooth out friction in the product experience.

Not all conversational bumpers are created equal. Some, like specialists, require a lot of resources to deploy, while others, like external messaging, require very little effort once they're set up.

I visualize conversational bumpers on a Care Continuum from hands-off to hands-on. There are six main types:

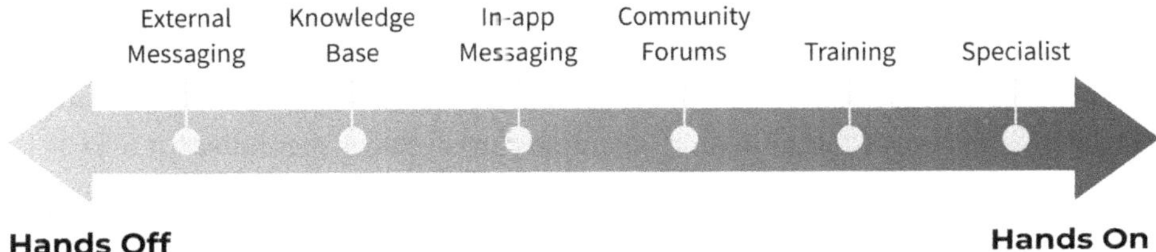

External messaging: These are texts, emails, LinkedIn connection requests—even snail mail! External messages should catch users wherever they spend their time. When users first sign up, they won't be immediately hooked and log back in every day. The best external messages also provide users with clear next steps.

Knowledge Base: Nowadays, most in-app chat solutions pair with a knowledge base. This means that a user can get an instantaneous answer to a standard question and quickly fix it, empowering them to solve problems independently (and deflecting support tickets).

In-app messaging: I love in-app messaging because sometimes you're struggling with something in an application, and you need to ask a very specific question. It's incredible when you can immediately message a company in-app and get a near-instant solution from a live representative. Even if it takes a few hours to get a response, it's still great to see there's a team behind the product that cares for its users.

Community Forums: Many software companies launch communities around their products. This is partly because communities can serve new users in better and different ways. Take Notion. You can use the product in many different ways, so a community where users share templates for how they're using the solution simultaneously increases adoption, engagement, and retention—a powerful combo.

Training: Let's face it: most software solutions require expertise to master. You can make your product incredibly easy to use, but you're missing out on a massive opportunity if you don't address the user's knowledge gap. This can come in the form of weekly coaching calls, an academy, or a live cohort that teaches users how to solve their biggest issues.

Specialists: Technical support specialists make it easier for users to hit the First Strike. Sales specialists help users make a business case for purchasing a solution. Specialists are by far the most hands-on you can be for users, but they can speed up the time your users get to value and upgrade. They also happen to be one of the easiest to start rolling out.

Depending on the average lifetime value of your customers, some conversational bumpers won't be sustainable (e.g., assigning everyone a specialist for a $10/month product). That said, optimize for being more hands-on at the beginning of your experience to accelerate learning.

You can always scale down your conversational bumpers once users get to value and upgrade on their own. You don't want your conversational bumper to feel like a "helicopter parent" doing everything for their child. That can turn away motivated users. Instead, act as a coach, providing guidance to keep them on track when needed.

If it's your first time building conversational bumpers, don't implement all six. Start by rolling out the "VIP experience." Give a select number of free signups the white-glove treatment. Let's say you have 40 signups per week. Reach out to everyone. Send them a quick welcome email, ask them to schedule an onboarding call, give them a trial extension if they need more time, or manually set up their account.

Do everything possible to get these users to experience the core value of the product and upgrade. Once you identify a winning pattern of activities, that's when you can roll out more scalable conversational bumpers (e.g., a manual welcome email could be automated, common questions answered during an onboarding call could be added to a knowledge base).

Do the unscalable tasks to optimize your learning about what makes users successful. Then, reverse engineer that process to give every signup the VIP experience.

Even with thousands of signups per week, offer VIP onboarding to high-value users. This helps your team understand exactly what users need to succeed, so you're not guessing. The unscalable path is how you identify the scalable path.

Create a Frictionless Onboarding Experience

Crafting an effortless experience takes a lot of effort. But it takes a lot less if you deploy the Bowling Alley Framework. Use the Bowling Alley Framework Canvas to unlock frictionless onboarding.

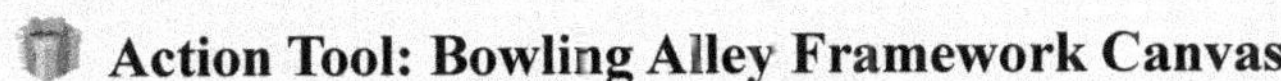

Action Tool: Bowling Alley Framework Canvas

Get your free Bowling Alley Framework Canvas at ProductLedPlaybook.com to help your users see value faster.

Download a
virtual copy here.

By starting with a straight-line onboarding journey, you typically slash 20 to 40% of steps that block users from value.

Once you've built your straight line, you can layer in a product bumper to make it dummy-proof for anyone to experience the core value of your product.

The conversational bumper will catch users where they are and assist them in whatever ways they need to succeed.

When you make your user experience effortless, you get rewarded with users who consistently engage with your product and are 10x more likely to become paid users.

And that's what's up next—pricing.

Company Name: ______ Designed by: ______ Date: ______

Bowling Alley Framework Canvas

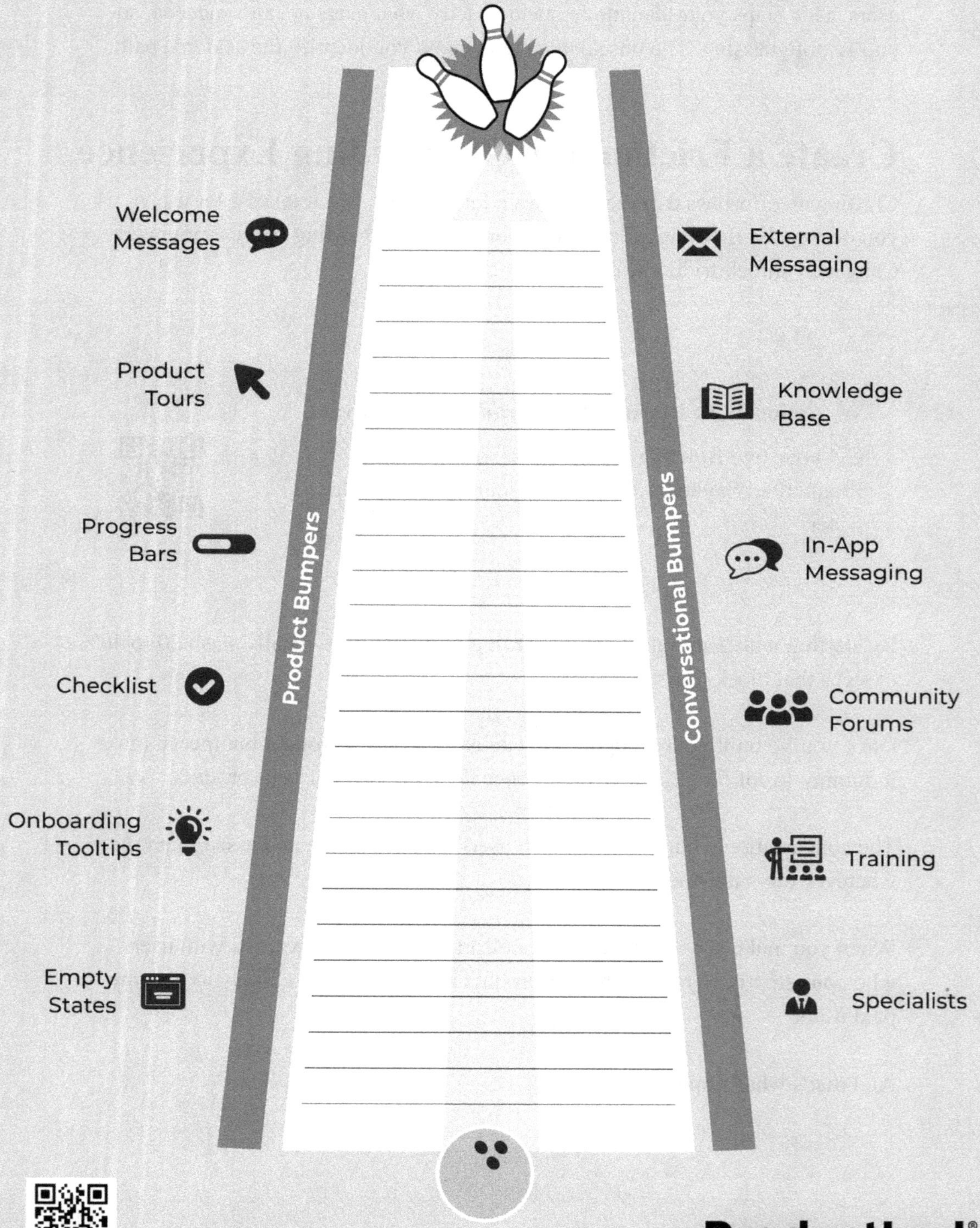

Product Bumpers

Welcome Messages

Product Tours

Progress Bars

Checklist

Onboarding Tooltips

Empty States

Conversational Bumpers

External Messaging

Knowledge Base

In-App Messaging

Community Forums

Training

Specialists

Download a virtual copy here

ProductLed®
productled.com

Actionable Takeaways

- 40 to 60% of first-time users visit your application once and never come back. Improving your first-time user onboarding experience is one of the most important things you can do. For a much deeper dive, read *Product-Led Onboarding: How to Turn Users Into Lifelong Customers* by Ramli John.

- Frictionless onboarding makes it effortless to sign up, get to value, and upgrade. You can design a frictionless experience by using the Bowling Alley Framework.

- To develop a straight-line onboarding experience, map out the fastest path to value, then triage every step to kill unnecessary ones, delay advanced ones, and pinpoint the must-haves. Those last ones are your straight-line.

- Product bumpers make it easy for your users to use your solution. Use them to direct users through your straight-line onboarding experience.

- Conversational bumpers catch users where they drop off and bring users back to the application. Use a more hands-on approach if you're in the early days of crafting your self-serve motion or are dealing with users that have a high lifetime value. Scale down to a more hands-off approach once you've identified what it *really* takes to help your users succeed.

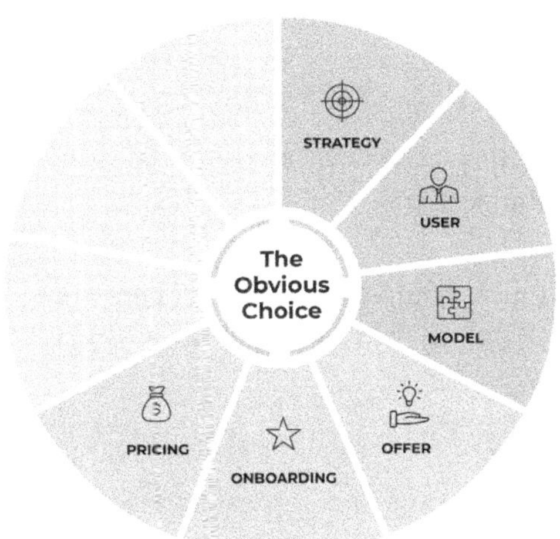

Powerful Pricing

How **well** do you turn free users into high-paying customers?

Subpar Great World-class

Rate yourself from 1 to 10.

A product-led business will die if it can't convert users into paying customers.

Getting users to upgrade is infinitely easier if you've created enormous value. Even if you do provide incredible value, it might not be enough to push users to pull out their credit cards and upgrade.

Your pricing must align your company's financial success with your user's success. When they win, you win—simple as that. This symbiotic relationship locks in incentives.

Take PromoTix: Every time a ticket is sold, PromoTix makes 1.75% of the fee. Sell 100 tickets, and you both win.

But great pricing isn't just about value metrics. There are several pricing traps that are all too easy to fall into. I would know. I've been ensnared by them all.

Trap 1: Not Being Transparent

If you go to a company's website and don't see the price…it's expensive.

A lack of transparency puts the user at a huge disadvantage. A user doesn't know if you'll charge them 10x the price of another user just because you have a more valuable use case. Sales-led companies can charge each customer a different amount. You could say this is good business. Yet the lack of transparency increases the time it takes to close a deal.

One of the easiest ways a company can build trust is by showcasing its pricing. This transparency sets clear expectations, speeds up decision-making, and leads to a quicker and smoother upgrade.

Trap 2: Misaligned Incentives

Your incentive as a business is to make more money. Your user's incentive is to maximize the value of your product. Great pricing aligns these incentives.

Symptoms of misalignment include difficulty increasing the lifetime value of a customer and flat revenue per user.

When incentives align, you'll make more per customer, which is great because one of the biggest benefits of a product-led business is to land and expand each account.

Let's say you run a merchant-of-record company like Paddle.com, and you currently charge based on features. Your Pro plan is $99/month, which gives a user the tools to charge international customers. Walmart.com signs up for your plan and processes $100 million in the first month.

Your team is scrambling. The amount of requests and support required to process that cash is overwhelming. You either have to cancel the customer or find a new pricing model.

A simple pricing model scales with the value your customers receive. In Paddle's situation, it's pretty simple. For every dollar a customer makes, you charge between 3 to 5% as a fee, like a credit card. When companies like Walmart.com sign up to use Paddle, you can support them as they scale up and remain incentivized to help them grow.

Trap 3: Big Jumps in Pricing

Product-led companies are land-and-expand machines. You might start charging users a small amount, but as users access more features and use your solution more, it's natural they'll be charged more.

Yet taking users from free to $2,000 per month is a steep jump few will make. Most companies with a steep pricing jump don't have a pricing metric that scales well, so they try to capture as much value as possible early in the relationship. This scares off a lot of potential customers.

This doesn't mean you can't charge $2,000 per month at some point; it just means you might start off with a small amount, like $50 per month.

Trap 4: Your Pricing Page is Confusing

Billions of dollars are lost each year on bad pricing pages. Even with well-bundled plans and aligned incentives, the complexity of pricing can still hamper conversions.

If users can't determine which plan is right for them in less than five seconds, your pricing page needs work.

Let's dig into the Value Ladder Framework so you can avoid these mistakes and turn users into high-paying customers.

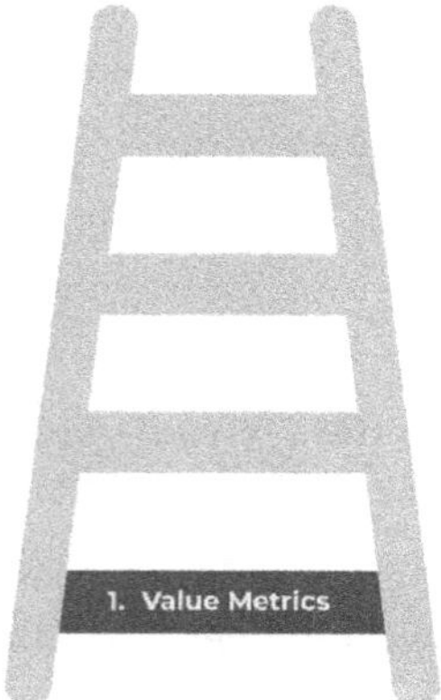

Phase 1: Identify Your Value Metrics

A value metric is the way you measure value exchange in your product.

Ultimately, value metrics are the linchpin of a product-led GTM strategy. You're aligning your revenue model with the success of your user.

Here's what they look like in practice:

- A value metric for a video platform like Vidyard could be the number of videos uploaded.
- A value metric for a communication application like Slack could be the number of users.
- For a payment processing platform like Paddle, a value metric could be the total revenue generated.

Patrick Campbell, former CEO of ProfitWell, emphasizes that value metrics outperform feature differentiation with up to 75% less churn.

Value metrics answer two key questions:

1. What does our ideal customer want in a product or service?
2. How much is the ideal customer willing and able to pay?

Value metrics represent what's needed to push customers to sign up, upgrade, or renew. You can also use them in reverse to determine why users remain on a free plan instead of upgrading.

A great value metric should be:

Simple to understand. When someone visits your pricing page, will they immediately know what they're paying for and which plan is best for them? For instance, if you're in the email marketing space, most solutions charge by the number of contacts, so using contacts as your value metric makes sense.

Aligned with the product's core value to the customer. For many companies, your value metric will align with the Key Usage Indicator (KUI) you identified in the User Component. For example, the KUI for practice management software might be when 25 appointments are booked. In this case, the value metric would be the number of appointments booked.

What core components lead someone to experience a meaningful outcome? The number of contacts in the CRM? The number of live-chat conversations started? Pieces of content downloaded?

Scalable. Does your value metric scale well? If users use 100 vs.10 units of your value metric, is it fair to charge them more? If customers get incredible value from your product, charge them more—your product is worth it. Charge customers less if they aren't getting the full value.

Although it's easy to suggest what makes a good value metric, choosing the wrong one is even easier.

How to Find Your Value Metric

Your value metrics help you monitor if users achieve meaningful outcomes in your product. They also play a critical role in reshaping your pricing strategy.

By now, you should have a few hypotheses about your value metric:

- Is it messages sent?
- Number of users?
- Revenue generated?

If you're in an established market, Greg Leach, a pricing consultant, recommends doing a market scan. The value metric is likely well-defined, and you'll benefit from using it versus trying to educate potential customers on a new one.

Review your Beginner, Intermediate, and Advanced levels from the Model Component and your KUI. One of the easiest ways to spot a value metric is to look at which items remain the same across all packages but have different numerical amounts.

To help you determine whether you should keep a value metric, take your top choices through the Value Metrics Scratchpad.

For example, Senja is a software company that makes it easy to collect testimonials. Should its value metric be the number of users?

Condition	True?
Is it simple for the customer to understand?	Yes
Is it aligned with the value the customer receives?	No
Does it scale with your customer's usage?	No

If Senja uses user-based pricing, they aren't aligning value with pricing. What if they used the number of testimonials collected as a value metric?

Condition	True?
Is it simple for the customer to understand?	Yes
Is it aligned with the value the customer receives?	Yes
Does it scale with your customer's usage?	Yes

In this case, as Senja customers collect more testimonials, Senja can charge them more. It feels right because it aligns the value they provide with the value the customer gets.

Limit your value metrics to one or two. Less is more.

Once you've identified your value metrics, it's time to package everything together.

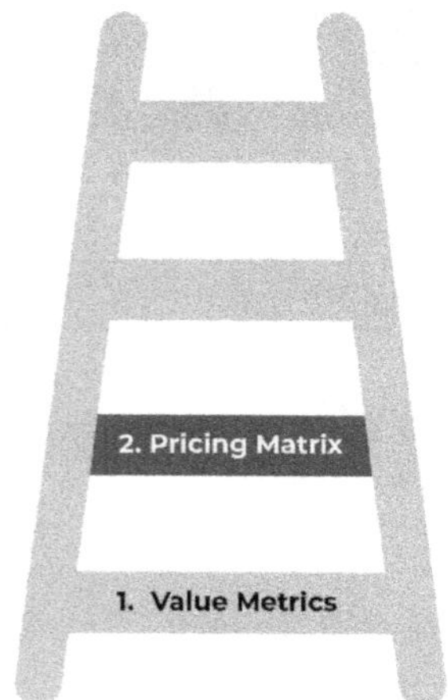

Phase 2: Build Your Pricing Matrix

Your pricing matrix is what users see on your pricing page.

Even if you showcased your pricing matrix and nothing else, they should be able to make a snap decision on which plan is right for them.

Your pricing matrix builds on the DEEP Model you created in the Model Component. It's the foundation for what goes into each plan. The main difference between the two is that the DEEP Model is used internally, while the pricing matrix is used externally.

Let's build off the PromoTix example from the Model Component.

Beginner Level	Intermediate Level	Advanced Level
Beginner Outcome: Publish an event page.	**Intermediate Outcome**: Sell more tickets with marketing tools.	**Advanced Outcome:** Save big on ticketing fees.
Challenges: • Ticket pricing. • Publishing the event page. • Payment processing and fees.	**Challenges:** • Marketing the tickets. • Creating graphics for event promotion. • Booking talent or artists to boost ticket sales.	**Challenges:** • Ensuring the event has the necessary features and services for attendees, such as RFID ticketing. • Ambassador program that meets the needs of promoters. • Create a mobile app.
Solutions: • Free event page builder. • Payment processing options. • Embed checkout. • Ticket inventory management. • Unlimited ticket types.	**Solutions:** • Mailchimp marketing email integration. • Google, Facebook, and AdRoll tracking pixels. • Event photo generator.	**Solutions:** • RFID wristband fulfillment, access control, cashless payments & sponsor activations. • Branded mobile app & app CMS. • Ambassador tasks and rewards.

This framework covers all the potential challenges a user will face when trying to set up and host a successful event.

While your pricing matrix will look very similar, there are a few important differences. The pricing matrix has a name for each level and a quick one-liner that indicates who each plan is for. It also includes a section for your value metric(s) and gives a high-level breakdown of features.

Ticketing	Ticketing + Marketing	Professional
For events that want a robust ticketing solution.	*For events that want additional marketing tools.*	*For professional venues, large festivals and events*
Free	$ /month	$$ /month
Includes:	Includes	Includes
• Free for event organizers who pass fees to attendees. • Unlimited ticket types. • Unlimited events.	• Everything in the Free plan. • Google, Facebook, and AdRoll tracking pixels. • Mailchimp marketing email integration.	• Everything in the Ticketing + Marketing plan. • RFID capabilities. • Mobile app CSS • Ambassador network access.
Get Started	Get Started	Get Started

A good pricing matrix gives users just enough information to make a decision. No more, no less.

Let's build yours.

Step 1: Name Your Plans

Don't get fancy. A generic pricing plan name is better than something that confuses users.

Some common plan names are:

1. Basic, Pro, and Advanced
2. Free, Starter, Professional
3. Starter, Business, Enterprise

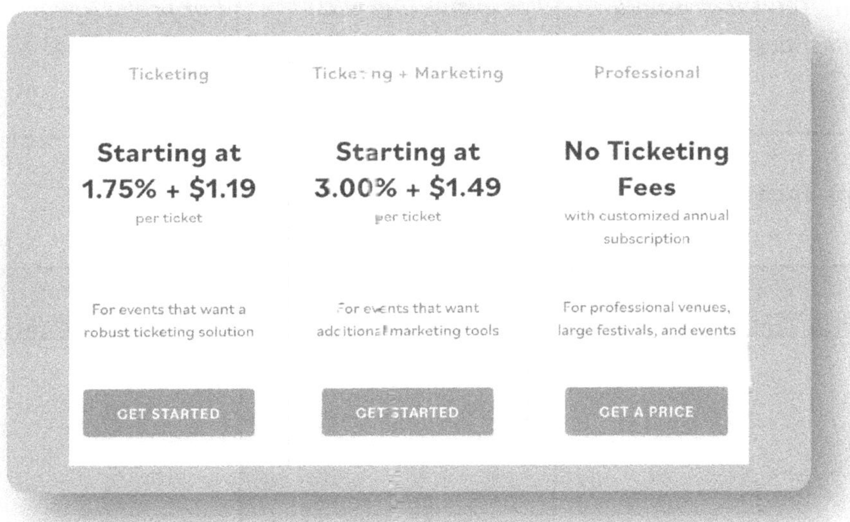

Even better, summarize what the plan enables you to do. For example, PromoTix uses Ticketing, Ticket + Marketing, and Professional as their three plan names.

Your Turn (To Fill In)

Beginner Plan Name	Intermediate Plan Name	Advanced Plan Name

Step 2: Write a Positioning One-Liner

Positioning copy does two things well. It tells the user:

1. Who this plan is for.
2. What it enables them to do.

Here's a good example from PromoTix.

Ticketing	Ticketing + Marketing	Professional
For events that want a robust ticketing solution.	*For events that want additional marketing tools.*	*For professional venues, large festivals, and events.*

Your Turn (To Fill In)

Beginner Plan	Intermediate Plan	Advanced Plan

Without this one-liner, you're asking too much of users. You'll fail the 5-second skim test—the amount of time it should take users to identify the right plan for them.

Step 3: Define What's Included

The hardest part of the pricing matrix is deciding what goes into each plan.

If you've filled out the DEEP Model, this should be a lot easier, but you'll still need to make some crucial decisions:

1. How much of any given value metric can I include in each plan?
2. Which features do I highlight on the pricing page?

Give users just enough information to understand what they're going to get without overwhelming them. Aim for no more than five features per plan. Ideally less. If users are super curious, you can always offer a full feature breakdown with a comparison chart below the pricing matrix.

List how much of any given value metric you're giving away for free. Make the value metric the first feature in this section so users can quickly scan each plan.

Ticketing	Ticketing + Marketing	Professional
For events that want a robust ticketing solution.	*For events that want additional marketing tools.*	*For professional venues, large festivals and events*
Free	$ /month	$$ /month
Includes:	Includes	Includes
• **1.75% + $1.19 per ticket** • Free for event organizers who pass fees to attendees. • Unlimited ticket types. • Unlimited events.	• **3.00% + $1.49 per ticket** • Everything in the Free plan. • Google, Facebook, and AdRoll tracking pixels. • Mailchimp marketing email integration.	• **No Ticketing Fees** • Everything in the Ticketing + Marketing plan. • RFID capabilities. • Mobile app CSS • Ambassador network access.
Get Started	Get Started	Get Started

If you have non-obvious features, underline some of them and add a tooltip that quickly explains the feature right on the pricing page.

Before moving on to the last step, decide:

1. How much of a value metric is included in each plan.
2. Which features are included in each plan, and which three to five to showcase. This should be closely tied to the solutions you built out in the Model Component.

Your Turn (To Fill In)

Plan	Value metric amount	Features to include
Beginner		
Intermediate		
Advanced		

Step 4: Call-to-Action

Lastly, list out the call-to-action (CTA) for visitors to take the first step.

For most product-led companies, this is typically "Get Started For Free," "Try For Free," or "Start Free Trial."

Make sure the next action is obvious and that every CTA is the same. However, you might want to say something like "Contact Us" or "Talk to Sales" for an advanced plan if you really do need to talk to them.

The CTA for the most popular plan should stand out with a high-contrast color (this is typically the middle plan).

Your Turn (To Fill In)

You have the skeleton of your pricing page. You're still missing one critical piece of information: the price.

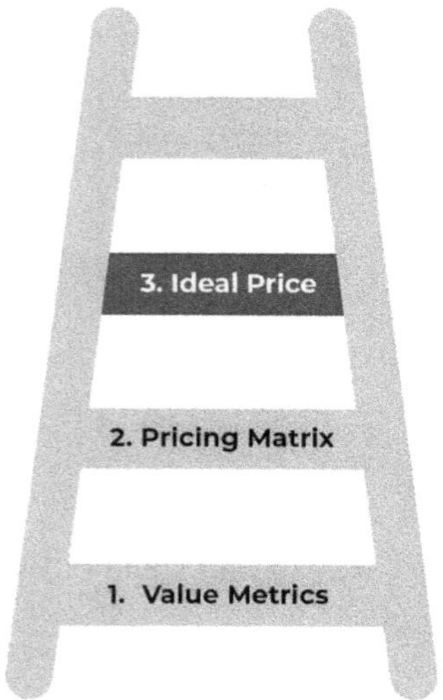

Phase 3: Determine the Ideal Price

One of the best ways to understand how much your customer is willing to pay for your product or service is to base your pricing on market and customer research.

The model I'm about to share with you is based on the Van Westendorp Price Sensitivity Meter. That's a bit of a mouthful, so we'll just refer to it as the 'Van West Model' from here on out.

This is the same model pricing experts at ProfitWell, OpenView, and Simon-Kucher use to help SaaS businesses nail their pricing. (I'm not sharing their proprietary method. This is simply one part of their framework.) The Van West Model will help you find an acceptable *range*.

Finding an acceptable price range is especially important because you want to avoid two disastrous consequences:

1. You set your price too high and lose out on most sales.
2. You set your price too low and lose out on most profits (while also hurting your brand, which appears "cheap").

You can figure out the acceptable price range in three steps.

Step 1: Choose a Plan

Don't make the simple mistake of sending out a pricing survey without being crystal clear on the plan it applies to.

Most product-led companies should start with their intermediate plan, as this has the greatest number of paid signups.

Step 2: Prep Your Pricing Survey

Pricing studies are dry for most founders, so let's give a fun example of how OpenAI used the Van West Model to nail down their pricing for ChatGPT Pro.

First, they asked free users to join a waitlist for their upcoming paid plan. After joining, they took you to a Google Form (nothing fancy).

Once there, they gave you a simple three-bullet overview of what the paid product would enable you to do.

ChatGPT Professional is geared towards professional use with:

- *Always available (no blackout windows)*
- *Fast responses from ChatGPT (i.e., no throttling)*
- *As many messages as you need (at least 2X regular daily limit)*

They stated that they might reach out to you if you'd like to upgrade.

They asked several key questions:

Question	Reason
What email address do you use for your account?	So they could dig into your usage.
What country do you reside in?	It shows how willingness to pay varies by country.
Please describe the most valuable thing you use it for.	For a horizontal platform where you can do anything in the product, this is especially useful to understand as people value different use cases differently.
Van West price sensitivity questions: 1. At what price ($ per month) would you consider ChatGPT Professional to be so expensive that you would not consider buying it? 2. At what price ($ per month) would you consider ChatGPT Professional to be priced so low that you would feel the quality couldn't be very good? 3. At what price ($ per month) would you consider ChatGPT Professional starting to get expensive so that it is not out of the question, but you would have to give some thought to buying it? 4. At what price ($ per month) would you consider ChatGPT Professional to be a bargain—a great buy for the money?	This helps them determine the ideal price point.
How upset would you be if you could no longer use ChatGPT (on a scale of 1 to 5)?	This is a classic product-market fit question developed by Sean Ellis, author of *Hacking Growth.* Yet, it serves a double purpose in a pricing study by segmenting results for the willingness of raving fans to pay vs. casual users.

For many early-stage companies, the ChatGPT example may be a tad overkill.

Most of you can get away with asking these five questions:

1. What's your email address?
2. What's your country of residence?
3. Please describe the most valuable thing you use our product for.
4. At what price ($ per month) would [our product] seem "expensive" (you'd have to think twice about buying it)?
5. At what price ($ per month) would you consider to be an "acceptable" price (good value for the money) for [our product]?

Kyle Poyar, Operating Partner at OpenView, introduced me to this simplified version with only two questions.

1. What would you consider to be an "acceptable" price (good value for the money) for [our product]?
2. When would [our product] seem "expensive" (you'd have to think twice about buying it)?

If you don't have many customers, use Kyle's method. You'll get more people to answer your questions, which is a challenge in itself.

Action Tool: Pricing Survey Template

We made a free survey template for you. Claim it at ProductLedPlaybook.com.

Download a virtual copy here.

Step 3: Who and How to Ask

The ideal people to ask depends on which plan you're trying to price. If you're trying to price your intermediate package, ask your ideal free users. If you're trying to price your advanced package, ask your intermediate plan customers.

Who you ask matters more than *how* you ask.

Your ideal users might value the product at 10x the amount that non-ideal users do. If you jumble up all the data, you could pick an ideal price range for everyone while missing out on landslide profits from ideal users.

So how do you ask them?

ChatGPT didn't even mention it was a pricing study. No one wants to fill out a pricing study. But who wants to join a waitlist for a new product? A lot more people!

How you frame this study is critical to getting more data. If you haven't launched this new plan yet or you're simply rebranding it from something like a "Pro" plan to another name, there's no harm in using the waitlist approach either.

How do you drive traffic to the survey?

1. In-app notifications.
2. Manually emailing free users who are a great fit.
3. Email notification asking for participation in a pricing survey.

Create a mini-marketing plan to get your pricing survey out to the right users so you can get solid data to pinpoint the ideal price range.

Step 4: Decide on Your Price

With the Van West Model, you want to create a graph with the data you've collected. The X-axis includes the prices people said they'd be willing to pay, and the Y-axis shows the percentage of people who selected each price range.

Pay attention to the points of intersection. Between the "Acceptable" and "Too Expensive" price ranges, the Optimal Price Point shows where people consider your product a good value. Don't charge less than that.

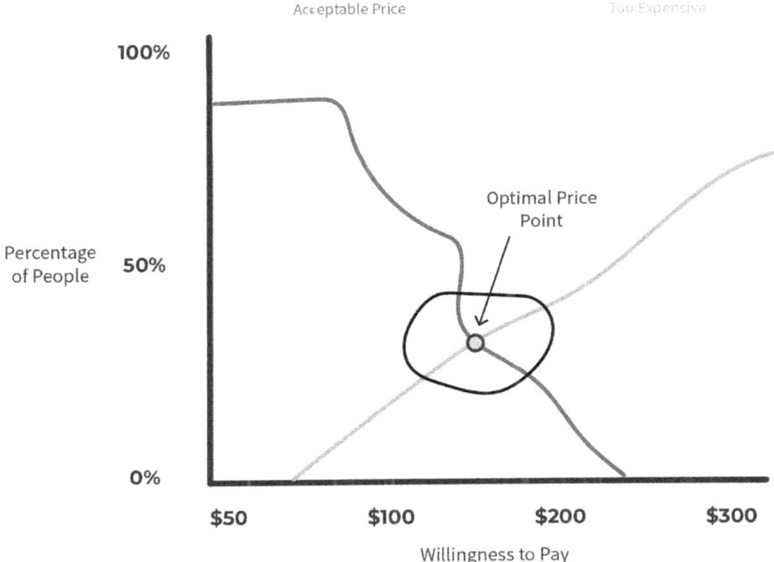

At the intersection of "Acceptable Price" and "Too Expensive," you'll find the Optimal Price Point. This is an excellent place to be—the point where people are most likely to buy.

Use these intersections to determine the pricing for each plan you offer.

Your Turn (To Fill In)

Beginner	Intermediate	Advanced
Free	$	$

We're on the home stretch. Let's refine your pricing page with all your new learnings.

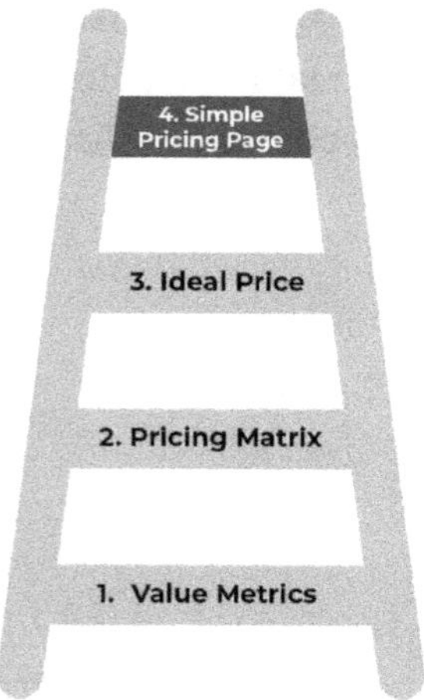

Phase 4: Build Your Simple Pricing Page

Have you ever loved a company's website and product only to get completely confused on the pricing page? It's disappointing—and more common than you think.

The gold standard for a pricing page is for users to be fully confident about the right plan for them in less than five seconds.

To do that, your pricing page must have three components:

1. A tagline that anchors your price: This could be when you present a high initial price on the left to make other prices seem more reasonable or attractive in comparison. Or include copy that positions your product against something that seems more affordable.

For instance, at ProductLed, we mention right before our pricing that hiring a ProductLed Implementer costs less than a single sales rep, yet unlocks a product that sells itself. Before you see our price tag, you're thinking of the cost of a sales rep. When you see the investment, it seems like a no-brainer. This is effective because without a price anchor, users are left to wonder if your price is a good deal.

2. Your pricing matrix: Add your ideal prices to the pricing matrix. You might want to add a pricing toggle to allow users to switch between monthly and annual pricing.

3. Frequently asked questions (FAQs): Most companies overuse the FAQ section. If everyone has the same question, it should be in the copy on your homepage. If some but not most people have a question, include it in your FAQ. If few ask it, cut it out. Use a chat bubble to prompt users to reach out if they have additional questions.

To boost conversions, consider the following (optional) enhancements:

Why choose your product: Remind users why they should choose your product. This adds healthy redundancy and reassurance. Users are on this page trying to make a buying decision—remind them they're making a fantastic choice.

Risk Reversal: Wherever your users sniff out risk, reassure them that everything is going to be okay. Choose the biggest risk and address it head-on.

Social Proof: Aim to have at least three pieces of social proof that relate to users' top three objections.

Now you're ready to put everything together in the Value Ladder Canvas.

Value Ladder Canvas

Company Name:

Designed by:

Date:

Price Anchor Tagline		
Beginner Plan Name	Intermediate Plan Name	Advanced Plan Name
Who It's For	Who It's For	Who It's For
Free	Price $	Price $$
Includes	Includes	Includes
Call-to-Action	Call-to-Action	Call-to-Action
Frequently Asked Questions		

Download a virtual copy here

Based on the book The Product-Led Playbook: How to Unlock Self-Serve Revenue and Dominate Your Market (With a Tiny Team)

ProductLed®

productled.com

Action Tool: Value Ladder Canvas

Grab our free Value Ladder Canvas at ProductLedPlaybook.com to follow along with this activity.

Download a virtual copy here.

Finally, your pricing isn't a one-off event. It should be something you consistently re-evaluate and update—it's one of the most important levers for your business.

Unlock Powerful Pricing

The Value Ladder Framework designs pricing that grows your customer value automatically. More importantly, your pricing is now simple, transparent, and strategic.

You'll have users who can sign up, get to value, and upgrade all on their own—something most sales-led companies can only dream about.

Welcome to self-serve customers.

Now, let's scale them.

Actionable Takeaways

- The four biggest pricing traps to avoid are: not being transparent, having misaligned incentives (where your user isn't getting more benefit from being charged more, or vice versa), big jumps in pricing, and a confusing pricing page.
- Value metrics form the foundation for any world-class pricing strategy. They align your revenue model with the success of your user.
- A pricing matrix should give a user everything they need to quickly decide which plan is right for them in less than five seconds.
- When identifying your ideal price, only run a pricing study for one plan at a time.
- To build a simple pricing page, you just need a tagline that anchors your price, your pricing matrix, and an FAQ. Everything else is a bonus!

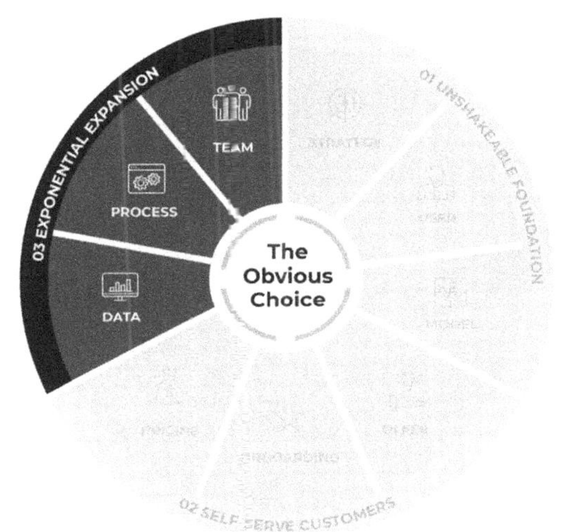

Stage 3

Ignite Exponential Expansion

Go from “linear” to “leveraged” growth.

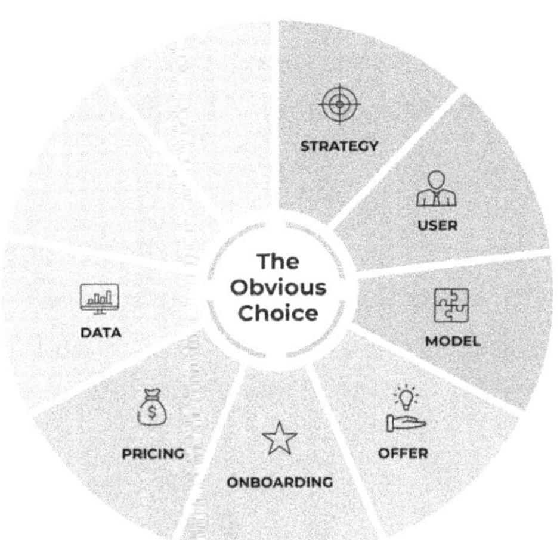

Actionable Data

How often are you **aware** of your #1 bottleneck in the business?

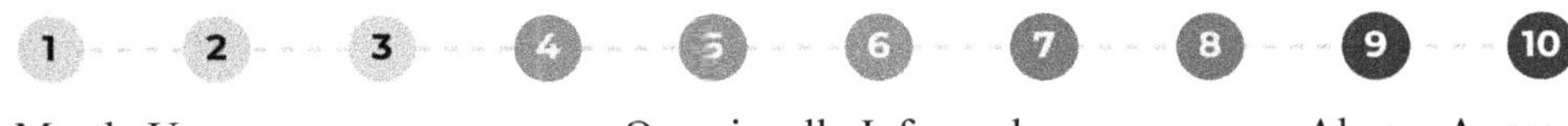

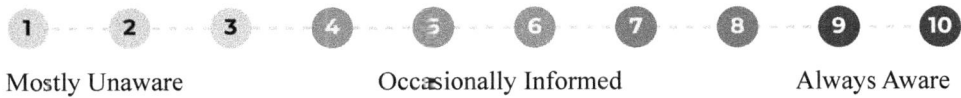

Mostly Unaware Occasionally Informed Always Aware

Rate yourself from 1 to 10.

Product-led companies must make data a core capability.

Unlike sales-led businesses, where talking to every potential customer is part of the sales process, you will not talk to most users. Just like body language tells us 55% of communication, what users do and don't do allows us to understand them without talking to them.

You need to understand if your users are getting to value—and, if not, pinpoint where they're getting stuck. In my experience, most product-led companies with a low free-to-paid conversion rate tend to jump straight to improving their onboarding experience.

In theory, that makes sense. Problem is, it's likely the symptom of a bigger issue. Remember that company I mentioned in the intro that spent one full quarter optimizing their onboarding with minimal results? When I dug into their data, I discovered a high volume of website visitors but a low sign-up rate.

So I went straight to their website. Their homepage lacked context on how the AI tool could solve a specific problem. Because of that, many visitors weren't likely to sign up in the first place. And those who signed up weren't motivated to use the product since they didn't know how the product could work for them.

No amount of onboarding improvements would save them. They spent months optimizing the onboarding experience when they should have focused on their offer. Imagine spending an entire quarter focusing on the wrong bottleneck!

This component is your guide to using data to identify what's bottlenecking your business at all times. You'll create a scorecard to focus your team on solving the top bottleneck. You need this data foundation before installing a predictable growth process in the upcoming Process Component.

As Jonathan Cronstedt, author of *Billion Dollar Bullseye,* notes, "No numbers, no business. Know numbers, know business."

Even if you think your metrics are nailed down, this component will simplify what you measure. Let's quickly go through four of the easiest data traps to fall into:

Trap 1: Tracking Everything

The first time we set up our scorecard at ProductLed, it was a Google Sheet with

36(!) metrics. Each metric listed someone who was accountable for it. We were a small team of five at that time, so some people were responsible for up to eight metrics. Our team didn't know where to focus, and we made little meaningful progress because our attention was spread thin.

Trap 2: No Accountability

When nobody is accountable for a metric, it often doesn't improve. Getting specific on who's responsible for every important metric will help you grow faster and identify accountability gaps affecting your ability to drive a metric forward (a great hiring opportunity).

Trap 3: Not Measuring What Matters

Should you track how many likes you get on your Instagram posts? How many impressions your videos get on YouTube? Some metrics might be important to look at occasionally. Far too many are vanity metrics—fun to track but with little connection to your business or users.

Trap 4: Not Segmenting Users

Unsegmented users are a mixed bag of analytics. "Mediocre" conversion rates might be great if you looked only at ideal users. An "amazing" marketing campaign might have recruited scores of bad-fit users. Segmenting your users is one of the best ways to understand the full story. Different segments have distinct needs, behaviors, and preferences.

Avoid these pitfalls, and you'll unlock three powerful outcomes:

1. **Total team alignment:** By being intentional with what makes it onto the scorecard, you clarify what matters most. This clear communication helps your team understand what's working and what's not.
2. **Peer-to-peer accountability:** Assigning ownership to each metric and reviewing them weekly builds a culture of accountability in which teammates hold each other to high standards.
3. **Accelerated growth:** With a focus on the biggest bottlenecks, your team can target and eliminate roadblocks faster, leading to fewer growth plateaus and a more rapid climb.

You can achieve all of this with the True North Framework.

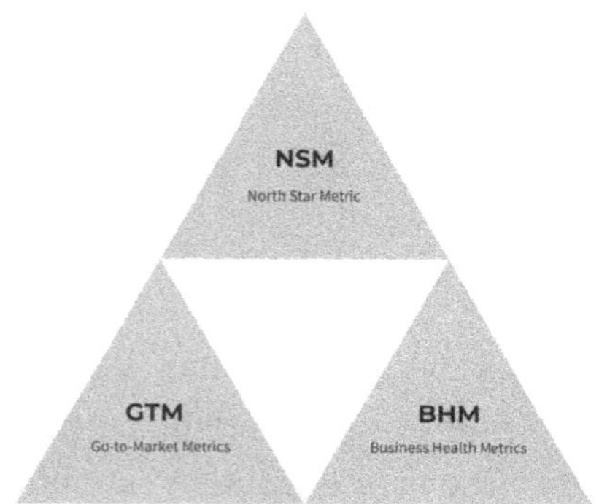

Phase 1: Identify the Core Metrics to Track

Imagine you're relaxing on a beach, finally disconnected from work. You can't help but wonder—should you extend your vacation or head back to the office?

You check your phone, where a simple scorecard shows a few key numbers. These numbers are the vital signs of your business. If they're solid, you know everything's on track and you can extend your vacation without worry. But if one flashes red, it's time to act—maybe even cut the vacation short.

This is the power of the "True North Framework." It distills your business down to its critical metrics, allowing you to understand instantly whether your business is thriving or if you need to intervene. With these numbers, you can confidently decide whether to relax or take action.

Track three core metrics:

1. **North Star Metric:** Identify one North Star Metric (NSM) and align your entire company around it.
2. **Go-to-Market Metrics:** Gain a holistic understanding of the user journey with a scorecard that easily tracks each step of the user journey.
3. **Business Health Metrics:** Understand how your business is *really* doing each week.

North Star Metric

A North Star Metric (NSM) captures the core value your product delivers. It aligns with your customer and company needs. Improvements to your NSM should also increase revenue.

Here are a few NSM examples.

Intercom	# of Customer Interactions Per Week
Salesforce	# Of Records Created Per Account Per Week
Zoom	# Of Hosted Meetings Per Week
Medium	# Of Minutes Spent Reading Per Week
Twilio	# Of Total Messages Sent Per Month
DocuSign	# Of Documents Signed Per Week
Airbnb	# Of Nights Booked Per Month
Uber	# Of Trips Booked Per Week
Instagram	# Of Active People Per Day
Slack	# Of Messages Per Week

Notice the alignment. With Airbnb, nights booked are a perfect NSM because when someone books a night, the customer, host, and Airbnb all win.

What Makes a Great NSM

For starters, the value of your company and the customer must be aligned. A revenue metric focuses only on what benefits the company. The number of times a user acts doesn't always tie back to company value.

If we dissect all the NSM examples above, they have three components:

1. **Quality metric:** An automated or manual action in your product (e.g., your product automatically fixes a bug on your customer's website, or they share a graphic they designed).
2. **Quantity metric:** Typically a number (i.e., how many times your user did a specific quality metric).
3. **Frequency:** How often you expect someone to do an action.

For Slack's NSM of "number of messages per week," the amount is the quantity metric, while messages represent their quality metric. If users are messaging each other, they're probably getting value from the product.

Frequency focuses on the cadence that makes the most sense for your users. For Slack, it makes sense that the frequency is weekly, as a standard workweek reflects the cadence of how you'd use the product. If you were to do a daily cadence, it wouldn't be as relevant—you'd always struggle to get more weekend engagement. For a product like Instagram, it's the opposite. They want you to use the product every day.

At Amplitude, a product analytics platform, they focus on the number of shared reports per week viewed by two or more people. They've dubbed this Weekly Learning Users. It shows them that users aren't just logging into their platform but are finding share-worthy insights, which is the quality metric.

If you're struggling to define your NSM, your value metric should be the leading candidate.

Let's say you run an email marketing platform and currently charge customers based on the number of subscribers. Your NSM could be the number of engaged subscribers per account. Your goal is to help these companies get more subscribers and engage them through great email marketing. As your customers gain more subscribers, you can charge them more because they derive more value.

If you're still struggling to define your NSM, it might actually be your Key Usage Indicator (KUI). Slack's KUI is when an account reaches its 2,000 message limit, so it makes sense for their NSM to be the number of messages per week. Your KUI and NSM are close cousins.

When your user does the NSM behavior, the user/customer gets more value, which helps your company capture more value (via higher retention or by charging more). This graph sums up a healthy NSM relationship between the user and the company.

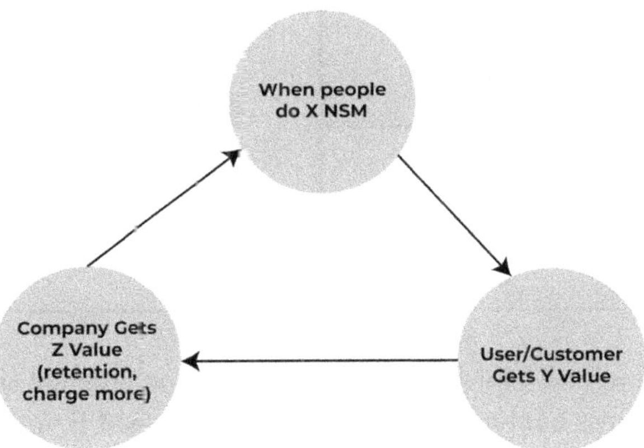

Your NSM should meet the following criteria:

- Is easy to measure.
- Correlates with your user's endgame.
- Is a behavior that your best customers do a lot in your product.
- It aligns with your company strategy.

The first time you choose your NSM, you might not be completely confident. That's okay. Pick an NSM and start tracking it. Over time, it will become obvious.

You can approach this from both the company and customer angle. From the company angle, look at the actions your highest LTV customers do consistently in your product. From the customer angle, look at what your best-retained users do consistently in your product.

Your Turn (To Fill In)

Potential NSMs	North Star Metric

Once you've found your NSM, your team will be more aligned and focused. However, you'll miss out on the true impact of your NSM if you don't use it effectively.

Go-to-Market Metrics

Your go-to-market (GTM) metrics reflect the key steps in your user journey. Although you could track all of the steps, we recommend focusing on six:

1. Unique visits to your website.
2. Signups.
3. Users who complete the setup.
4. Users who complete the first strike.
5. Users who complete the KUI.
6. Users who upgrade.

These metrics represent the key steps of your user pathway (identified in the User Component).

You can almost immediately pinpoint the bottleneck. Say you're getting plenty of visitors and signups, but only 1% make it through the initial setup step. Where should you focus your team's efforts? Onboarding.

One of our clients had 7,300 monthly visitors but only four signups. The bottleneck was obvious—improving the signup conversion rate. Doubling site visitors wouldn't have solved anything.

Even if you don't have the right tooling to track all of these metrics, track as many as you can. Resist the urge to add a bunch of other nice-to-have GTM metrics. Less is more.

Business Health Metrics

Nothing else matters if your business runs out of money.

Keep your eye on three metrics:

1. Monthly Recurring Revenue (MRR).
2. Total Revenue Churn.
3. Cash Balance.

You're probably tracking your MRR and Total Revenue Churn already, but I doubt you're tracking your cash balance on a weekly basis. A cash balance tallies all the cash your company has in its accounts.

At ProductLed, we asked our bookkeeper to track our cash balance on a weekly basis. We soon realized that although we were making good sales, we weren't actually improving our cash position because we were unknowingly adding expenses at the same rate as revenue.

In less than six months of tracking this metric, we cut our annual expenses by more than $300,000. This might not be a lot of money for some businesses, but it made us much more profitable.

If you want to include some secondary business health metrics (BHM), consider:

1. Net Revenue Retention: Measures recurring revenue after factoring in expansions, downgrades, and churn.
2. Expansion MRR: Tracks additional revenue from existing customers through upsells or cross-sells.
3. Average Revenue Per Customer: Calculates the average income generated per customer.
4. Customer Acquisition Costs: The cost of acquiring a new customer.

Don't get FOMO and add everything. The BHMs you choose should be like the gauges on your car dashboard—just enough information to know what's going on.

Your Turn (To Fill In)

Business Health Metrics

Compile your core metrics into a snapshot document. Remember: There are no revolutionary metrics. Change comes from how you use them to make decisions.

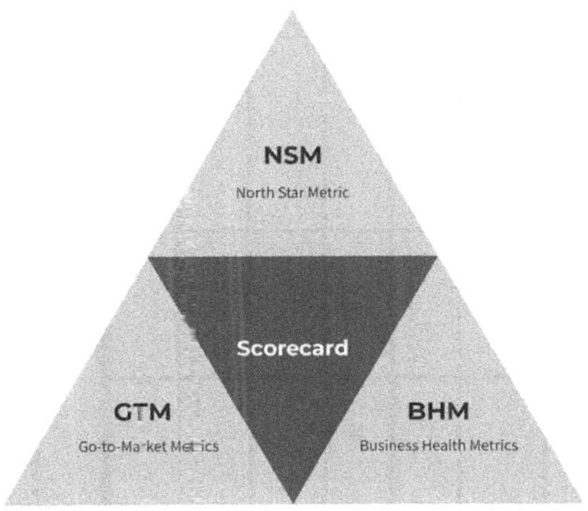

Phase 2: Build Your Weekly ProductLed Scorecard

Your ProductLed Scorecard is a simple spreadsheet that your entire team can easily view and contribute to.

Place all of the metrics you identified in Phase 1 into the scorecard.

To take your scorecard to the next level, layer in accountability. For every metric, assign an owner who passes the Ownership Test:

- ☐ Will they be able to make a **big impact** on this metric?
- ☐ Do they **want** to own this metric?
- ☐ Do they have the **capacity** to own this metric?

According to EOS® Worldwide, these three questions ensure you're putting the Right Person in the Right Seat.

A dedicated owner ensures each part of your customer journey has someone responsible for improving a key metric. Since it's a weekly scorecard, it guarantees that it's a top priority.

It's also great for your team because it makes it easy for them to know where they stand. Everyone deserves to know whether they're doing a great or poor

ProductLed Scorecard

Company Name:

Date:

	Week 1	Week 2	Week 3	Week 4	Remainder	Monthly Actual	Monthly Target	Status	Metric Owner	Metric Source
North Star Metric										

Go-To-Market Metrics

	Week 1	Week 2	Week 3	Week 4	Remainder	Monthly Actual	Monthly Target	Status	Metric Owner	Metric Source
Visits										
Signups										
Setup										
First Strike										
Key Usage Indicator										
Upgrades										
Churned Customers										

Business Health Metrics

	Week 1	Week 2	Week 3	Week 4	Remainder	Monthly Actual	Monthly Target	Status	Metric Owner	Metric Source
Monthly Recurring Revenue										
Total Revenue Churn										
Cash Balance										

Download a virtual copy here

Based on the book The Product-Led Playbook: How to Unlock Self-Serve Revenue and Dominate Your Market (With a Tiny Team)

ProductLed®

productled.com

job. Before you assign random monthly targets for new metric owners, have each owner backfill the ProductLed Scorecard for the previous month. This will require them to identify where they can track their metric, confirm that they can track it, and give you a baseline for a realistic weekly target.

Action Tool: Free ProductLed Scorecard Template

Grab our free digital ProductLed Scorecard at ProductLedPlaybook.com.

Download a
virtual copy here.

By design, the ProductLed Scorecard is filled out manually. Entering the data yourself encourages deeper thinking about why a metric is off or how to better achieve a goal. Of course, this can be tough if your data is buried in a complex data warehouse, hence the need for a simple product analytics tool, but we'll save that chat for later.

Your ProductLed Scorecard creates weekly opportunities to talk through how to get the most out of your product—and the team that manages it.

What I love most about the ProductLed Scorecard is that whoever owns an off-track metric basically becomes "CEO for the week." Their metric becomes everyone's top priority, and they can enlist the full support of the company to turn it around. Over time, this creates a collaborative culture and allows metric owners to attack their metrics relentlessly.

In the Process Component (up next), we'll unpack when and how to review your ProductLed Scorecard.

Phase 3: Install Product Qualified Leads

Product Qualified Leads (PQLs) are an advanced metric. Start using your ProductLed Scorecard for at least a month before adding in PQLs. They can be more challenging to track if you don't have product analytics in place.

A PQL is an ideal user who has successfully set up their account, received the core value from your product, and hit a KUI. You want PQLs because their odds of upgrading are high—30 to 50%.

If you've defined the stages of your user journey and implemented profiling questions into your onboarding flow, you have all of the ingredients to track PQLs:

- Ideal User Profile: Is this your ideal user? Ask profiling questions during signup, such as "What's your job title?"
- Successful Setup: Have they completed the setup stage? For some tools, this could be installing a script.
- First Strike: Have they experienced tangible value? This is the first moment a user realizes how your product can help them.
- Hit a KUI: Are they forming a habit with your product? Do they experience the core value frequently?

When used correctly, PQLs:

- ☐ Incentivize your marketing team to drive ideal signups.
- ☐ Simplify who your customer success team should assist first in the free experience.
- ☐ Clarify who's ready to upgrade to a paid account.

Every team can play a part. PQLs align your team's success with your user's endgame.

How to Rollout PQLs

The best part about PQLs is that you need to make only a slight modification to the six core metrics you track in your GTM Metrics. Essentially, you segment your data to focus on tracking your ideal signups and you swap out KUIs for PQLs.

Here's what it looks like:

Without PQLs	With PQLs
1. Unique visits to your website.	1. Unique visits to your website.
2. Signups.	**2. Ideal Signups.**
3. Users who complete the setup	3. Users who complete the setup.
4. Users who complete the first strike.	4. Users who complete the first strike.
5. Users who complete the KUI.	**5. PQLs.**
6. Users who upgrade.	**6. Ideal users who upgrade.**

One of the recurring themes of this book is that your user's success ultimately becomes your success. By ensuring teams align to help your PQLs, you do just that.

Access Actionable Data

The True North Framework provides a simple approach to understanding what's *really* going on in your business, where the bottleneck is, and who owns what.

Yet, creating transparency, ownership, and accountability for core metrics isn't enough. You need constant triggers to prompt teams to review their metrics and unlock peer-to-peer accountability.

We'll dig deeper into how to review your scorecard consistently in the Process Component.

Whenever an owner hits their target, publicly praise them. This is a new behavior you want to have on the team. It's also an excellent opportunity to ask the owner what contributed to this success.

The gold standard is to always know what's holding your company back so that you can invest your team's time in attacking that gnarly bottleneck. The ProductLed Scorecard simplifies this process by eliminating guesswork and providing you with a dashboard to run your business effectively.

What do you do when you identify your bottleneck? That's the Process Component.

Actionable Takeaways

- Each time you add another metric to track to your scorecard, you water down your focus. Less is more.
- You've chosen the right NSM behavior when the user gains more value from doing it, which helps your company capture more value through higher retention or increased pricing.
- Review your ProductLed Scorecard weekly with your leadership team to identify what the biggest bottleneck is in the business.
- Whoever owns a metric that is off track becomes the CEO for the week in that they call the shots and can enlist the support of the rest of your leadership team to attack their metric and turn it around.
- Use this formula to define what a PQL is for your business: Ideal User Profile + Successful Setup + First Strike + Hit a KUI = PQL
- Every team in your company can and *should* play a small part in increasing the number of PQLs your company has every week.

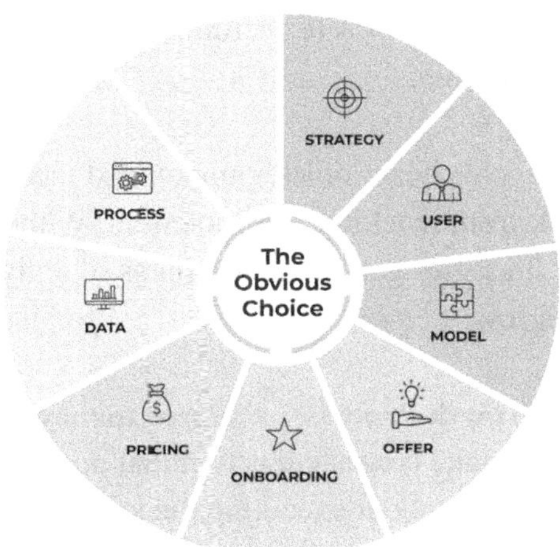

Growth Process

How well does your company translate **action into results**?

Inconsistent Effective Flawless

Rate yourself from 1 to 10.

Execution makes you the best, even if you're not the first.

Apple didn't invent the portable music player; they perfected it with the iPod. Google wasn't the first search engine; they provided the best results. Electric vehicles existed before Tesla; Tesla made them desirable.

The same goes for your business. To win, you must out-execute everyone. It takes relentless focus to turn your strategy from theory to practice—and it's where most companies stumble.

Challenges like unclear goals, team misalignment, and inconsistent execution hold organizations back from reaching their potential. Without a structured process, even the best strategies get lost in the chaos of daily tasks, scattering teams, and stalling progress.

Enter the **Predictable Growth Process**—a simple framework to help your team stay focused, aligned, and take consistent action that *actually* makes an impact. It's not about doing more; it's about executing the key initiatives that drive growth.

It revolves around three core meetings that transform how your team operates. These meetings create a rhythm that enables your company to move faster, execute better, and stay laser-focused on the goals that will make the biggest impact.

At the top, there are **Strategic Alignment Meetings (SAM)**. These quarterly, high-level sessions sharpen your long-term strategy and ensure every department—from product to marketing—is on the same page. They are about stepping back to assess your progress, refine your strategy, and ensure that the entire leadership team aligns with the upcoming quarter's goals.

Next, there are **Monthly Focus Meetings (MFM)**. This is where strategy becomes action. You'll break down your quarterly goals into a focused, 30-day plan that ensures 80% of your team's efforts drive toward one goal.

Note: I highly recommend not facilitating these two meetings yourself. When planning your quarter and month, you want to be laser-focused on identifying your top priorities—not managing the process. Don't dilute your focus when it counts.

Finally, **Weekly Accelerator Meetings (WAM)** keep the momentum going. These quick, high-energy check-ins provide the accountability and clarity needed to make every week a step toward your monthly goals. These meetings help identify bottlenecks, resolve issues, and ensure your team is executing with precision.

🎁 Action Tool: High-Impact Meeting Templates

Grab your free templates at ProductLedPlaybook.com to run these high-impact meetings with your team.

Download a virtual copy here.

Together, these meetings generate disciplined execution, tight alignment, and consistent progress. They're the backbone of the Predictable Growth Process, and they're how you translate action into results—fast.

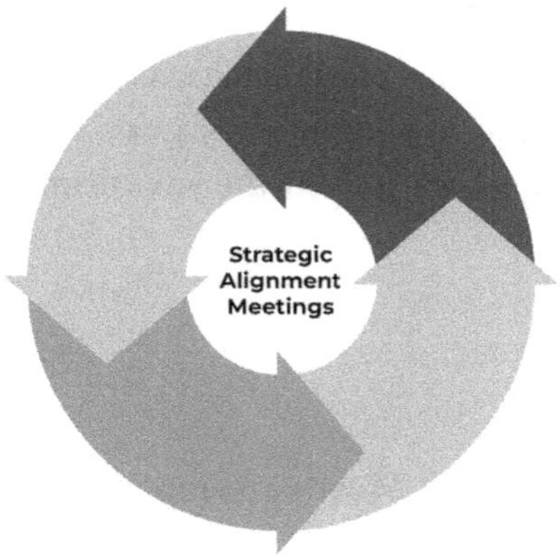

Strategic Alignment Meetings

These quarterly and annual meetings provide a strategic overview and ensure the leadership team aligns on long-term objectives while setting the focus for the upcoming quarter. SAMs allow for a broader review of progress against the One-Page Endgame (OPE), ensuring that all departments, including product and engineering teams, are synchronized with the company's long-term goals.

Here's the meeting structure:

Who: The leadership team and department heads (including Product, Engineering, Marketing, Sales, etc.). Ideally, there should be no more than 10 team members.

Facilitator: ProductLed Implementer (so the leadership team is 100% focused on discussions)

Duration: Full-day

Frequency: Quarterly. Please note this quarterly meeting will replace your MFM (i.e., you won't hold a SAM and MFM in the same month).

Prep: Review the OPE, update the ProductLed Scorecard with quarterly results, and list strategic priorities and issues.

Here's a typical agenda:

Check-in (15 minutes): To kick off the meeting, jot down everyone's expectations for this planning session. You'll get honest feedback here, and often, you'll get a clear idea of issues or goals for the quarter ahead.

Retro (30 minutes): This is a reflection on the past quarter. It combines a general retrospective with a focused review of your top initiatives. Start by asking your team these three key questions:

- **What went well?** Reflect on the successes of the past quarter. What initiatives, strategies, or actions led to positive outcomes? Celebrate the wins and recognize the efforts that contributed to achieving them.
- **What didn't go well?** Identify the challenges and obstacles that hindered progress. Were there any missed opportunities or areas where the team fell short? Understanding what didn't work is crucial for learning and improvement.
- **What to do differently?** What strategies, processes, or actions should change in the upcoming quarter to better achieve your goals? Based on the above reflections, determine the adjustments needed to improve moving forward.

This combined reflection helps the team gain insights from the past quarter and sets the stage for more informed decision-making in the upcoming quarter. Any issues that arise can be added to the issues list to discuss further (more on that below).

Strategy Review (30 minutes): Review your OPE. After every section, ask your team if they still believe this is the best path forward. The first few times you review your strategy, you might change your moats, clarify your ideal user, and nail down some strategic choices. This is completely normal. Your OPE is a living document that will evolve as your company scales.

Accountability Chart Review (30 minutes): You'll build this out in the Team Component (up next), but this is where everyone is clear on who's responsible for what and where the gaps are. Go through at least one cycle of your growth process before adding in the review of the accountability chart.

Scorecard Review (15 minutes): Review the ProductLed Scorecard you built in the Data Component. Every team member should fill out their metrics before the meeting and mark them with one of five statuses:

1. On Track
2. Trending on Track
3. Off Track, Have a Plan
4. Off Track, No Plan
5. Off Track, No Plan, Target Unreachable

If there's a plan, the expectation is that they link to it, create an issue, and review it with the team. Great (or up-and-coming) leaders will showcase how they can own a metric by creating a plan of attack when it's off track. If the metric is off track with no plan or the target is unreachable, note it as an issue to discuss later in the meeting.

This is peer-to-peer accountability at the highest level.

Targets (10 minutes): Clarify the targets for the upcoming quarter. Start with your 1-Year Picture and Quarterly Picture. Decide on the Top Outcomes (typically, your revenue, revenue per employee (RPE), and profit).

Review each metric in your ProductLed Scorecard and set targets to make your 1-Year Picture and/or Quarterly Picture inevitable. This gets everyone on the same page. For instance, if you had only 100 customers in the past quarter but set a new target of 200, make sure marketing is also in agreement to double the number of ideal users.

Top Goals (20 minutes): Once you've got a good handle on the main issues and where to focus, list out the top goals for the quarter. Make these SMART goals. Aim for no more than 3 to 5 quarterly goals, as each additional goal slows down your team. It's better to have less and complete them early than try to do too many things simultaneously.

Once a year, you'll set annual goals as well. But for the rest of the SAMs, you'll need to set just your quarterly ones.

Issues (90 minutes): At this point in the meeting, you will have consistently identified issues to address. For instance, if you're not getting many customers and don't have a plan, add that as an issue. If some mission-critical projects weren't completed last month, that's an issue. If your team hasn't been able to address its top bottleneck in the past month, note it here.

This is your time for discussion and to plan the best path forward.

Component Deep Dive (30 minutes): This is a deep dive into *one* of the ProductLed System components. For example, has it been 12 months since you updated your strategy? Refresh it by going through the Strategy Component again. Lacking clarity on your ideal user? Review the User Component. Not getting enough signups despite strong traffic? Tackle the Offer Component again.

The ProductLed System is not a set-it-and-forget-it method. Think of each component as a plant. You need to water and maintain it to reap fruit.

Top Focus (30 minutes): Now that you know exactly what you're doing for the upcoming quarter, you can set *one* Top Focus for the month ahead—the highest-leverage opportunity in your business. It might be:

- Improve customer retention.
- Improve the first-time user experience.
- Increase signups.

The top bottleneck from your scorecard is a big hint. But uncovering your highest-leverage opportunity isn't formulaic. You need to look beyond the numbers. Sometimes, what's not being done is holding back your growth.

For instance, if fewer users are signing up, why? Because your offer isn't positioned correctly? Because it's confusing? Whatever you decide is your highest-leverage opportunity is only a guess, albeit a data-backed one.

Top Projects (30 minutes): Identify the Top Projects for the month ahead, starting with those that directly address the Top Focus. These are the projects that, when executed, will make reaching your targets inevitable. Ensure these projects have a clear path to impact your business' highest-leverage opportunity.

Additionally, any other projects not directly tied to the Top Focus should still contribute to achieving your quarterly targets. It's crucial that every project contributes to measurable outcomes and is aligned with the organization's broader goals.

Go one step further and quickly break down success for each:

- Who will own it?
- Who's responsible for executing each aspect?

Add these projects to your project management tool. Everyone should aim to have no more than five Top Projects.

Cascading Messages (5 minutes): Reinforce the focus for the next month so the rest of the company is aligned. Consider hosting an all-hands meeting, sending a recap email, or using another method to ensure everyone is informed. Redundancy is beneficial as it reinforces top priorities.

Conclude (5 minutes): To wrap up, ask:

1. Were expectations met?
2. How would you rate the meeting on a scale of 1 (terrible) to 10 (outstanding)?
3. Any feedback to improve next time?

Jot down the answers.

Don't skip this step, even if folks are tired. You'll gain valuable feedback on how to improve these meetings next time.

You can use our template to host your Strategic Alignment Meetings.

Strategic Alignment Meetings

Company Name:

Designed by:

Date:

Check-in

Targets

Component Deep Dive

Cascading Messages

Top Focus

Retro

Top Goals

Conclude

- Expectations
- 1-10 Rating
- Feedback to Improve

Top Projects

Review

- Strategy Review
- Accountability Chart Review
- Scorecard Review

Issues

Download a virtual copy here

Based on the book The Product-Led Playbook: How to Unlock Self-Serve Revenue and Dominate Your Market (With a Tiny Team)

ProductLed®
productled.com

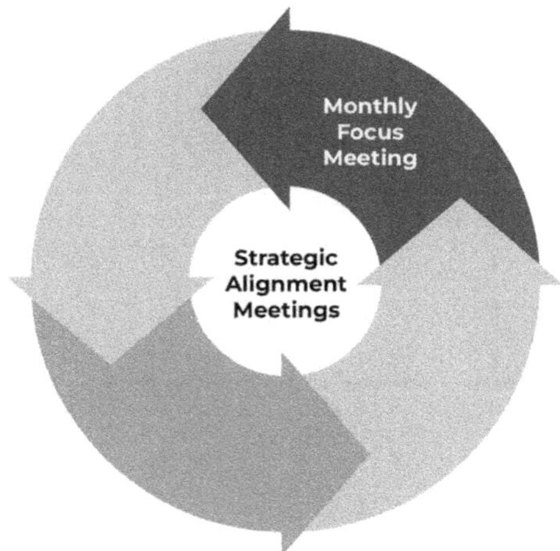

Monthly Focus Meetings

These are fantastic meetings to step out of the day-to-day, examine your business' performance, and decide what to do next. MFMs give everyone on your leadership team time to work *on* the business, not *in* it.

Planning is a muscle. Holding these meetings every month ensures the team stays focused on achieving their targets, driving consistent progress toward business goals. By maintaining this cadence, you can tackle short-term challenges while keeping your long-term strategy on track.

Here's the meeting structure:

Who: The leadership team

Facilitator: ProductLed Implementer (so the leadership team is 100% focused on discussions).

Duration: Half-day

Frequency: Monthly.

Prep: Strategic Alignment Meeting, update the ProductLed Scorecard, list out Projects & Issues to discuss.

Here's what a typical agenda looks like:

Retro (15 minutes): This is a critical reflection on the past month and should not be skipped. It's an opportunity for the team to have an open and honest conversation about what worked, what didn't, and how confident everyone feels about hitting quarterly targets.

Ask your team to answer these three questions before the meeting and add them manually on the call. It sounds like extra work, but it shows your team you recognize their ideas.

1. What went well?
2. What didn't go well?
3. What to do differently?

The Retro isn't a formality—it's where the team can extract valuable learnings from the past month and identify adjustments for the upcoming month.

Top Focus & Project Review (30 minutes): Go through each project you defined the month before to ensure it's done (unless this is your first time). If something isn't done by the end of the month, it's off track. It sounds obvious, but you'd be surprised how many teams still mark tasks as on track when they're weeks late.

Also, review if you've made a dent in your quarterly Top Focus. If not, add it to the issues list. You want to dissect whether or not you identified the right highest-leverage opportunity or if you're simply not executing well.

Scorecard Review (15 minutes): Review the ProductLed Scorecard and ensure every team member fills out their metrics before the meeting and marks them with one of the five statuses discussed above. If the metric is off track with no plan or the target is unreachable, it should also be noted as an issue.

Targets (10 minutes): Start by updating what your Monthly Picture looks like in your OPE. Then, go through each metric in your ProductLed Scorecard and set targets that make your Monthly Picture inevitable. If there are any issues, add them to the issues list for discussion.

Issues (45 minutes): This is your chance to address any issues that will hold you back from hitting your targets and making your 1-Year and Quarterly Pictures a reality.

Top Focus (10 minutes): This one will look familiar since you've already completed a cycle of this during the SAM. Set *one* Top Focus for the month—the highest-leverage opportunity in your business.

Remember, your scorecard's top bottleneck offers a clue, but you need to look beyond the numbers. For instance, if fewer users are upgrading, is it because your pricing is confusing?

Top Projects (20 minutes): Again, this will look familiar since you'll have done this during a SAM meeting. Each team member should bring a list of projects that they believe are key to roll out for the upcoming month. Each one should support your monthly Top Focus.

To prioritize projects, ask:

- Which projects will have the biggest impact on our Top Focus?
- Which projects will best help us hit our Targets?

Once the projects are identified, prioritize them based on cost and impact. Go one step further and quickly break down success for each:

- Who will own it?
- Who's responsible for executing each aspect?
- What's involved with rolling out each project?

Add these projects to your project management tool. No one should have more than five. Let your team know it's okay to pivot or kill projects that become irrelevant.

Cascading Messages (5 minutes): Consider hosting an all-hands meeting, sending a recap email, or using another method to ensure everyone outside of your leadership team is informed of the company's Top Focus and Projects for the month.

Conclude (5 minutes): To wrap up, ask:

1. How would you rate the meeting on a scale of 1 (terrible) to 10 (outstanding)?
2. Any feedback to improve next time?

Meetings, not just KPIs and products, need to get better, too.

You can use our template to host your Monthly Focus Meetings.

Monthly Focus Meetings

Company Name:

Designed by:

Date:

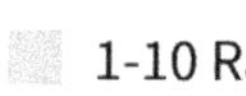
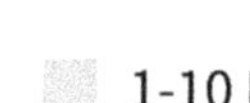

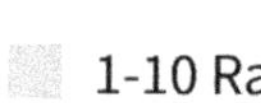
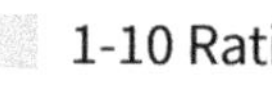
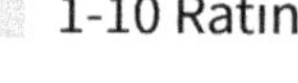
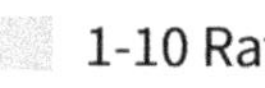
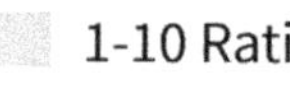
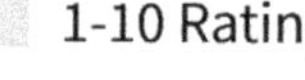

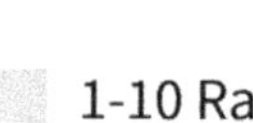
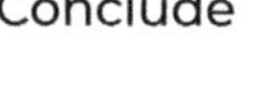
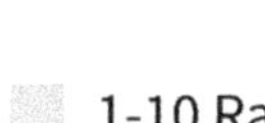
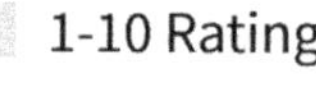

Retro

Review

- Strategy Review
- Accountability Chart Review
- Scorecard Review

Targets: Monthly Picture

Issues

Top Focus

Top Projects

Cascading Messages

Conclude

- 1-10 Rating
- Feedback to Improve

Download a virtual copy here

Based on the book The Product-Led Playbook: How to Unlock Self-Serve Revenue and Dominate Your Market (With a Tiny Team)

ProductLed®
productled.com

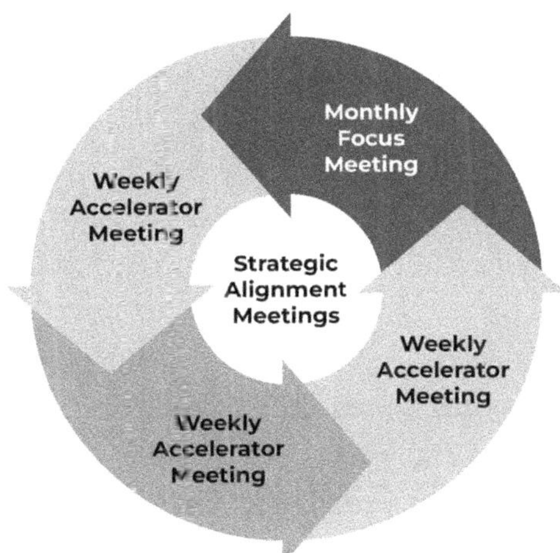

Weekly Accelerator Meetings

These are weekly meetings that give everyone a chance to check on alignment, track their progress, and address any issues. They are crucial to ensuring everyone stays on track.

Here's a quick rundown of the meeting structure:

Who: The leadership team

Duration: 90 minutes

Frequency: Weekly

Prework: Monthly Focus Meetings, update the ProductLed Scorecard and Top Project progress

Here are the main agenda items you'll cover in the WAM:

Wins (5 minutes): Share one personal and professional win. This starts the meeting off on a high.

Monthly Picture Review (3 minutes): Take a few minutes to review the Monthly Picture and see if you are on or off-track. This aligns everyone on the team with the company's top focus and the outcomes for the month before getting into tactical details.

Scorecard Review (3 minutes): Be quick. Ask everyone who owns a metric whether it's on or off-track. If anything is off-track and there's not already a solid plan in place, add it to the issues list.

Project Review (3 minutes): Review everyone's projects by asking them for a simple on or off-track update. If a critical project is off-track, add it as an issue to discuss.

To-Do Review (3 minutes): If you identified specific to-do's in a previous WAM, review them to see if all are marked as done. Most to-dos don't get done because people forget. Putting this on the agenda increases peer-to-peer accountability and ensures that what's planned is executed.

Issues (60 minutes): Before your meeting, you should have jotted down specific issues to discuss. As you go through the first five items above, you'll often find several issues. Triage which are critical and use the same format in the MFM to identify the root cause.

Top Three Priorities & To-Do's (10 minutes): This is a simple check-in to review everyone's top three priorities for the week and helps the entire team know who's doing what, increasing collaboration and accountability. Ideally this is captured in your project management application for reference at the next WAM.

Rating (3 minutes): Rate the meeting from 1 to 10 and share feedback on how to improve it.

You can use our template to host your Weekly Accelerator Meetings.

Weekly Accelerator Meetings

Company Name: ______ Designed by: ______ Date: ______

Wins	Issues	Top Priorities and To-Dos	Rating
☐ Personal ☐ Professional			
Review ☐ Monthly Picture Review ☐ Scorecard Review ☐ Project Review ☐ To-Do Review			

Download a virtual copy here

Based on the book The Product-Led Playbook: How to Unlock Self-Serve Revenue and Dominate Your Market (With a Tiny Team)

ProductLed®
productled.com

Now that you know the three key meetings for driving predictable growth, schedule them to recur weekly, monthly, and quarterly. This creates an unstoppable rhythm that keeps your team aligned on the long-term vision while being laser-focused on executing today's most impactful projects.

Make Speed Your Key Differentiator

In today's competitive markets, it's not the big that eats the small—it's the fast that eats the slow.

Companies that drag their feet on execution lose their edge and get copied. It's not just about turning strategy into action. You need speed to win. You need speed to capitalize on your strategy.

The Predictable Growth Process empowers your team to swiftly turn strategy into focused execution and stay ahead of the competition.

By aligning on the vision each quarter, locking in key projects monthly, and making massive progress every week, you gain the edge to outpace competitors, adapt quickly, and unlock predictable growth.

Actionable Takeaways

- Execution is the ultimate differentiator. It's not enough to have the best strategy in your market. You must become the best at capitalizing on it.
- Your meeting rhythms control the pulse of your business. During tough times, your business should pulse faster. During smooth sailing times, you can slow down the pulse rate to focus on initiatives that take longer to execute.
- Your Strategic Alignment Meetings (SAMs) are the most important meetings in your entire company. They shape your company's future and chart the best path to reach your goals.
- Monthly Focus Meetings (MFMs) keep your team focused on the top priority and ensure 80% of work aligns with it.
- Weekly Accelerator Meetings (WAMs) align your team on what the main focus is for the rest of the week and help address any hairy issues head-on.
- Although you can host your own Strategic Alignment and Monthly Planning Meetings, it pays dividends not to. A ProductLed Implementer can facilitate these meetings for you so you can focus your mental energy on what the highest-leverage opportunity is and the most effective way(s) to address it.
- Speed is the ultimate long-term competitive advantage.

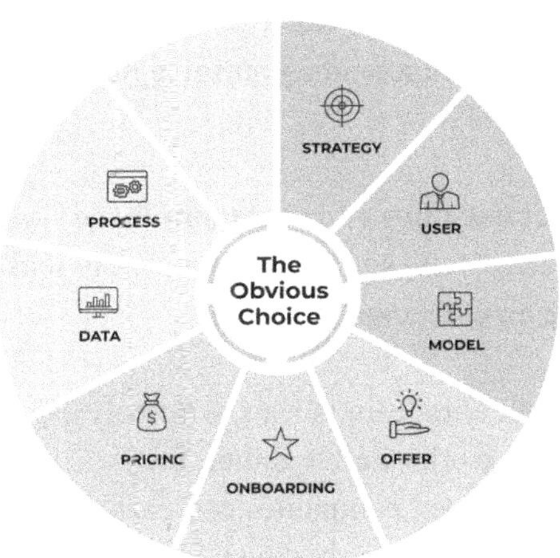

Elite Team

Does your team have **what it takes** to become the obvious choice in your market?

Barely Capable Somewhat Capable Unstoppable

Rate yourself from 1 to 10.

Userflow hit $5M ARR with just three employees. (And, no, they didn't have any contractors–I asked.) That's over $1.6 million in revenue-per-employee (RPE).

A high RPE is a hallmark of great product-led companies. Why? Because the product does all the heavy lifting—from onboarding to value creation, support, and upgrades.

It's also why product-led companies can afford to hire as a last resort. By implementing all the prior components, you solve most problems with your product.

Over time, your product **becomes your best employee**—your best salesperson, support rep, and marketer. However, to become the obvious choice in your market, you must have an elite team.

Like a top sports team, an elite team is lean, with only essential roles. Each member is highly skilled, works well together, focuses on results, and constantly improves. But most product-led companies can't afford to hire top talent with proven experience (at least in the early days). You need to build a team that can grow and evolve as your company scales.

I won't cover hiring strategies here, but I highly recommend reading *Who: The A Method for Hiring* by Geoff Smart and Randy Street for insights on recruiting top talent.

By the end of this component, you'll know how to design an elite, lean team, raise performance standards, and quickly level up your existing team. Let me introduce you to the **Elite Team Flywheel (ETF)**.

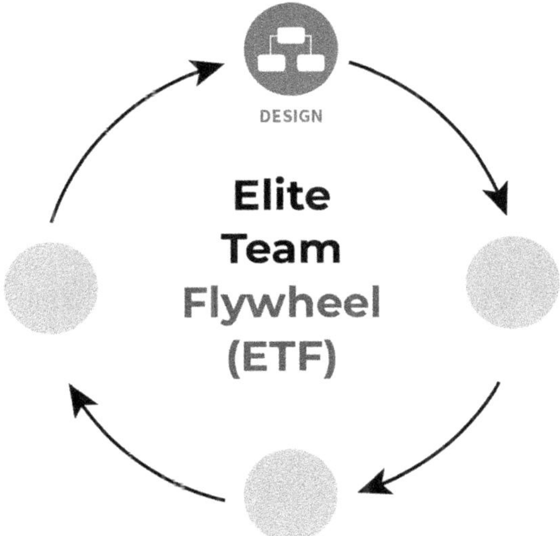

Phase 1: Design the Team

Start designing your team with an accountability chart. An accountability chart is a visual tool that defines roles, responsibilities, and reporting relationships.

It's similar to an organizational chart but with one distinction: One person can own more than one job. For instance, your Head of Product might also be the Head of Finance, as well as the website manager.

Without breaking down each job, you'll look to hire expensive unicorns who can do many things. Finding someone great at social media advertising, operations, and finance, for example, is hard compared to finding someone to handle just social media advertising.

Traction by Gino Wickman introduced me to accountability charts. It was a game changer for our business. We knew who was accountable for what and realized that underperformance was almost always because someone was doing too many jobs.

Build your chart from the top down. In EOS®, they recommend unbundling the CEO job into two roles:

1. The Visionary is the person with the creative ideas. They set the vision and establish the business's values, strategy, and culture.

2. The Integrator is the COO or CTO-type who approaches the business systematically. An Integrator turns the vision into reality.

In solo-founder companies, the same person wears the Visionary and Integrator hats. However, as the company grows, these often become separate jobs—very few people can be a true Visionary and brilliant Integrator.

Who is the Visionary, and who is the Integrator on your team?

Your Turn (To Fill In)

Role	Team Member
Visionary	
Integrator	

Next, list the other main jobs required to help your business grow. For most product-led companies, this is someone in charge of owning the GTM motion and product.

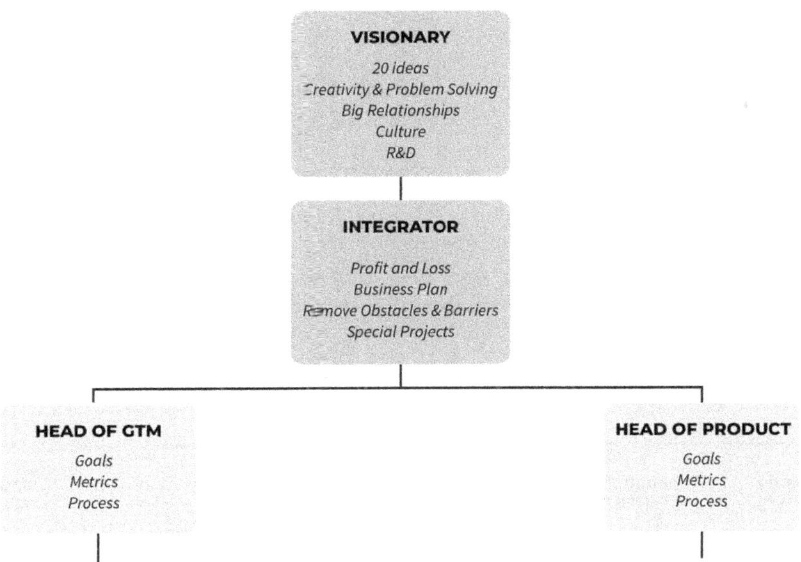

These are the most important areas of a product-led business. Your GTM leader gets the product out into the market while your Head of Product crafts the product around your customers' needs.

These don't have to be your leadership roles, but it's a simple place to start.

Your Turn (To Fill In)

Role	Team Member
Head of GTM	
Head of Product	

Once you've identified your leadership team, go a layer deeper and list all the supporting jobs.

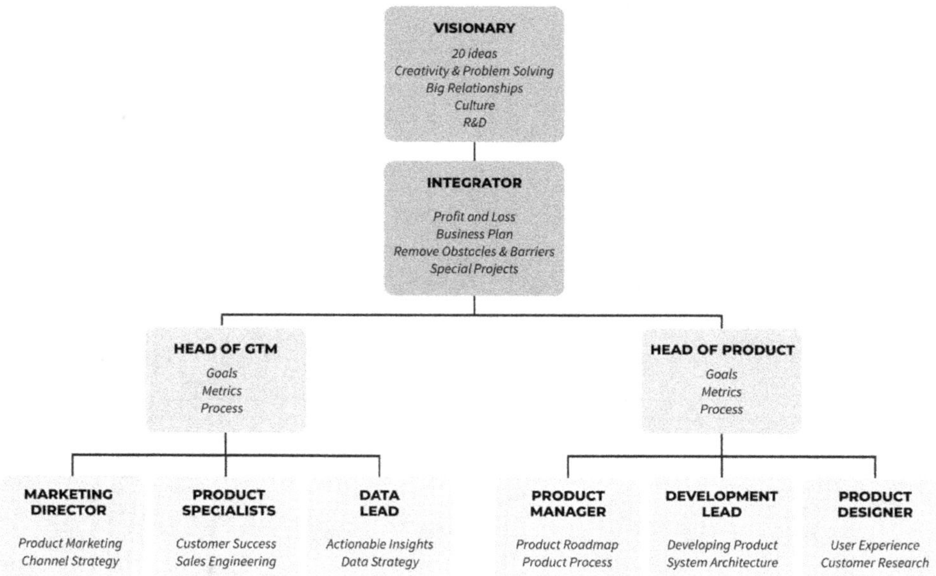

Don't get caught up in titles; they're for reference only. What matters is what you put below—specifically, the responsibilities assigned to each job. This keeps the ego out of the activity.

Ensure the core capabilities you identified in your OPE are well represented. If not, build these capabilities out soon to bring your strategy to life. You may also realize that you have capabilities on your accountability chart that you no longer need.

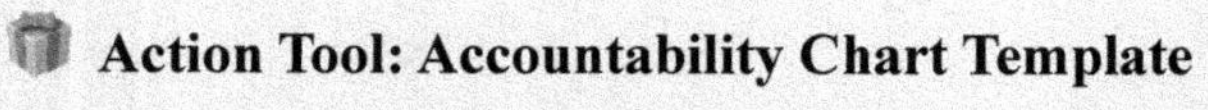

Action Tool: Accountability Chart Template

You can grab our free template to build out your accountability chart at ProductLedPlaybook.com to understand the responsibilities of your team.

Design a Lean Team

Of all the listed jobs, which are required?

One of my favorite triage tools is the 3T system from Mike Michalowitz, author of *Clockwork*. Here's what each T stands for:

1. Trash: You can safely eliminate the job without impacting anything. Never worry about this again.
2. Transfer: This job is important but needs to be transferred. Who can do it better?
3. Treasure: This job is critical to the business and needs to be protected. How can you dedicate more time to it?

Each step leads to pruning. Analyze your jobs based on these three Ts.

You should eliminate 10 to 20% of jobs that are no longer required. Like a sports team, each role needs to be 100% intentional. Having three goalies is silly, but how often do you have two or three people doing a job that should be handled by a specialist?

Review your accountability chart during every SAM to clarify who owns what and eliminate jobs.

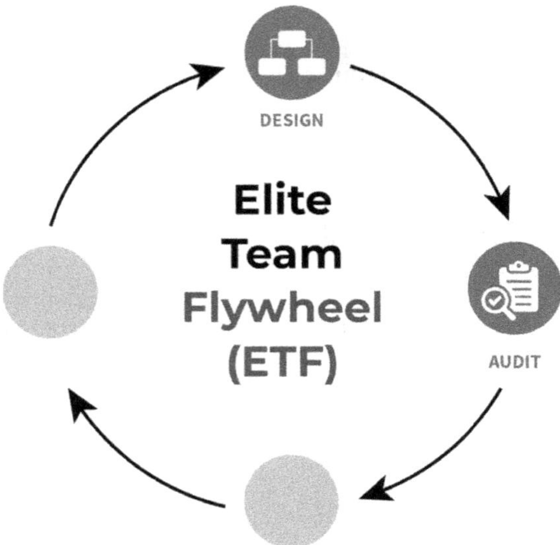

Phase 2: Audit the Team

Auditing your team can feel scary, but it's necessary to raise the bar for performance. There are two ways to do it.

Like a computer virus scan, there's a quick scan and a full performance scan. One checks the most important stuff; the second checks everything. Having both options allows you to address team issues faster.

Quick Audit

The quick audit makes hiring and firing decisions 10x faster.

Use the core values from your OPE to build your quick audit criteria. Do you want someone on your team who doesn't align with your core values?

Create a checklist to analyze each employee and contractor to see if they meet your core values—always, sometimes, or never.

You can use the quick audit at other times, too:

- Ask it in an interview: Can you give me an example of how you embody X core value?
- Use it as a checklist to decide which candidate best fits a new role.

- Complete it in the first week or two of hiring a new team member to validate they embody your core values.
- Review it before a new employee's probationary period ends.
- Assess it when you think someone is not the best fit for your team.

Let's run three employees through a quick audit.

Say your core values are Simplicity, Energy, and Drive.

To simplify the scoring, use (+) to indicate always, (+/-) to indicate occasionally, and (-) to indicate never.

Team Member	Simplicity	Energy	Drive
Sarah	-	-	+/-
Josh	+/-	+/-	+/-
Melissa	+	+/-	+

Sarah rarely has good energy and complicates tasks. She has two areas where she never embodies the core values and is an okay fit in the other. She likely should be let go.

Josh, on the other hand, is a mediocre fit in all core values. He doesn't meet the criteria, so he should be let go, too.

Melissa is almost a perfect team player. You might decide to coach her on managing her energy, but other than that, she's a great fit.

You might also have some non-negotiables to add to this list, like Integrity. That is up to you and the type of organization you want to build. The goal is to raise the bar for your team, so making choices about who to keep is absolutely part of this activity—and it's the hardest part.

If you're still unclear about who to keep on your team, complete a more thorough performance audit.

Performance Audit

Your quick audit helps you identify who's a fit for your team. Always run the quick audit before a performance audit, as you can quickly screen out folks who are a bad fit.

The performance audit takes time to complete but gets to the bottom of performance issues.

Use it when:

- You have someone on the team who is underperforming.
- You want to raise the bar on your team's performance and proactively address performance issues.
- Someone owns more than three jobs.

One of the biggest challenges with assessing performance is that one person might be doing five jobs. They're great at one, okay at three, and below standard on another. This is common at resource-strapped startups—everyone's wearing multiple hats.

As an organization grows, it's normal for employees to shed jobs as the standards for each gets more focused.

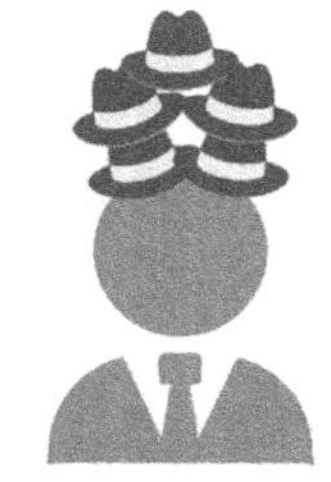

To analyze someone's performance fairly, you need to audit each job. It's unfair to let someone go simply because they're wearing too many hats.

Use these four key markers to determine whether someone is right for each job:

1. Motivation: Do they *really* want the job?
2. Results: Do they *consistently* hit their targets?

3. Skills: Do they have the *required* skills to do their job?
4. Capacity: Do they have the *capacity* to do this job?

Pick one person and one job they do. Do this *with* the team member so you can understand all their jobs.

Let's go back to Melissa since she passed the quick audit.

She currently has three jobs:

1. Social media manager
2. Copywriter
3. Email marketer

Social media management represents most of her time, so audit that job first. She's highly motivated, gets results, and has the skills required, but surprisingly, she doesn't have the capacity to dedicate enough time to it.

For her copywriting job, you learn that she's motivated to do it and occasionally gets results but lacks the skill to do it effectively. She doesn't have much capacity to do this job well either.

For her email marketing job, you learn that she's not motivated to do it, and although she generates results and has the skills, she still lacks capacity.

Use (+) to indicate yes, (+/-) to indicate occasionally, and (-) to indicate no.

Team Member: Melissa				
Jobs	**Motivation**	**Results**	**Skill**	**Capacity**
Social Media Management	+	+	+	-
Copywriter	+	+/-	-	-
Email Marketer	-	+	+	-

Melissa could delegate the email marketing job to a more motivated team member and train them, freeing her to focus on social media management and copywriting.

She lacks the necessary skills to succeed as a copywriter, so you can put a training plan in place to level her up. It makes sense to invest because she's genuinely motivated to get better.

Our graphics designer at ProductLed is a perfect example of how well this can work. She started helping our team with administrative tasks but mentioned she'd like to learn more about graphic design. She has blown us away over the past two years with her skills. Every week, she gets better at her craft.

When someone is motivated, they quickly build skills, dedicate more time to the job, and deliver results.

Before you complete a performance audit, I challenge you to complete one for yourself. Odds are, you're doing too many jobs and aren't the right person for all of them.

Your Turn (To Fill In)

Team Member:				
Jobs	**Motivation**	**Results**	**Skill**	**Capacity**

You've set the performance bar. Now raise it.

Raise the Bar for Performance

Your audit reveals high performers and mediocre ones. What you decide to do will be different in every business, but here's a decision tree to make this part easier:

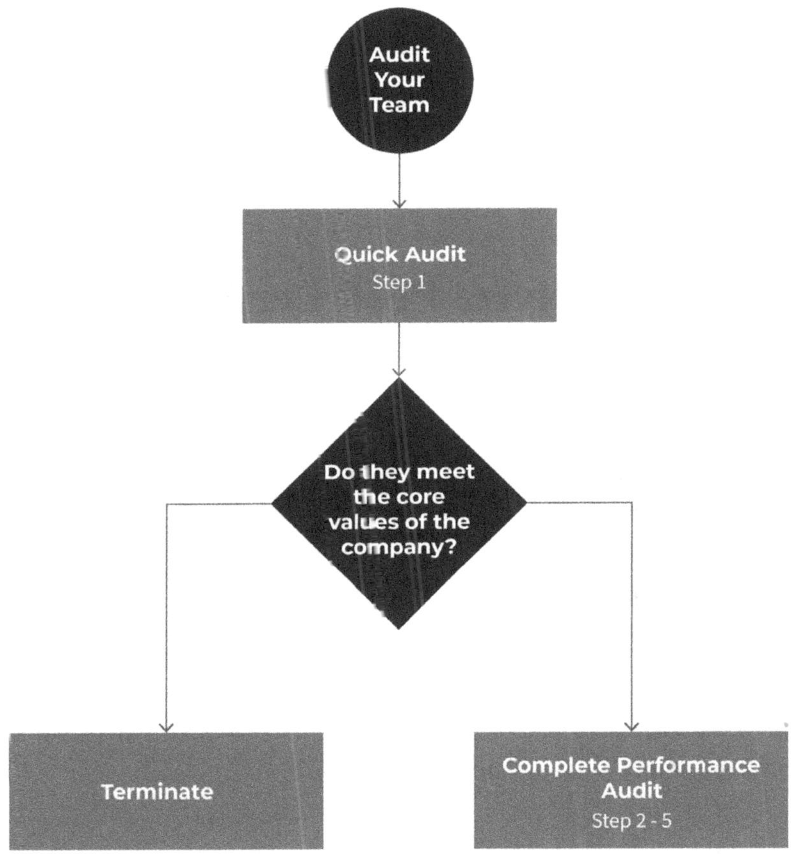

If someone doesn't align with your core values, you need to make the tough call and remove them. If they meet your core values, then move on to the performance audit.

If you go through this decision tree and consistently audit your team, you quickly raise the standards and build a high-performance culture.

Yet even if you do all these things, you might still have underperforming A-players. Why? The incentives aren't right.

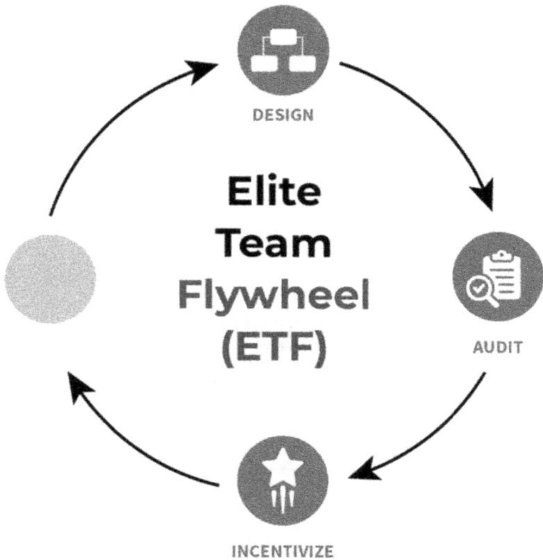

Phase 3: Incentivize Peak Performance

Peak performance starts with smart incentives. Motivated individuals build a motivated team.

There are endless ways to incentivize—many of them overly complex. I'll focus on one: unlocking motivation.

Incentivize Individuals

Assuming you pay a decent wage and have good benefits, how do you unlock the peak performance of every individual on your team?

Ask them a question: What is your 5-year vision?

You may need to help them crystalize this vision.

- What do you want to be earning?
- What do you want to be doing?
- What does your ideal work/life balance look like?
- What does success look like?

The minute you can align their vision with what they're doing everyday, your "employee" is no longer working for you. They're working for themselves.

You unlock a whole new level of productivity in them. They'll go the extra mile to push their vision forward because it benefits both of you. Win-win.

When you critique them, tie it back to their vision and how improvement will help them realize it faster.

This can also have the opposite effect. Sometimes, when an employee is clear on their vision but it doesn't align with the company, you have to part ways. But at least you know why and can create a transition plan that works for everyone.

Ask each of your direct reports about the big vision for their career that excites them. Keep checking in to help them craft that vision.

Incentivize the Team

In your OPE, you unpacked the endgame for your business.

This is the equivalent of winning the Super Bowl for your company. When football teams win the Super Bowl, it's a big deal. Yet when most companies hit their endgame, it's a secret—and the founder might be the only winner.

Elite teams are different in that they love to win. You design an elite team to make your endgame a reality. What's the incentive for your team to smash your quarterly or one-year winning picture? To achieve the endgame?

Let's say you have a profit target of $1 million. Would your team be more incentivized to hit that target if 10% of that profit was shared in a team profit pool? Of course!

You also need markers of progress. For instance, if your endgame is serving 10,000 customers in the next five years, what happens at 1,000 or 5,000 customers? This can be a one-time reward (e.g., a company retreat in an exotic location) or a recurring incentive (e.g., profit sharing).

What makes winning great is that something is at stake. If you don't win, you lose out. If you win, you unlock something you didn't have before.

When you master incentives, you:

1. Align your entire team with the company's success.
2. Increase employee engagement.
3. Improve retention rates.
4. Attract top talent.
5. Boost team collaboration.

This creates a culture in which everyone aligns with the company's top goals and has skin in the game to achieve their individual goals.

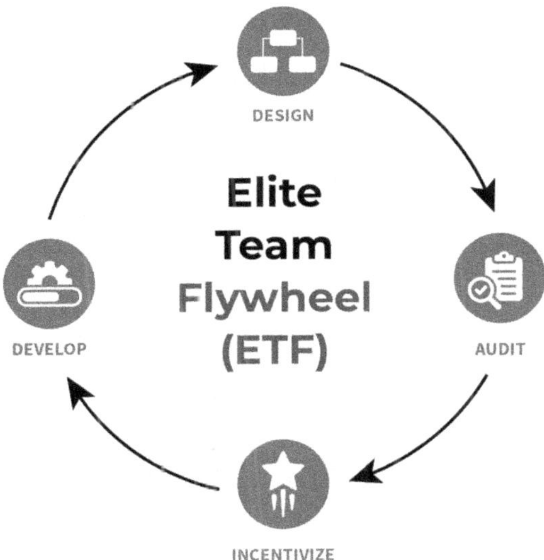

Phase 4: Develop Unstoppable Capabilities

In your OPE, you identified key capabilities your business needs to win. These can't be outsourced—they must be built and developed in-house.

What makes capabilities unstoppable is constant growth within the teams that own them. Neglecting to train top talent is a missed opportunity. Without new skills, your team will plateau. The best teams always invest in upgrading their capabilities.

Team development is one of the most underrated leadership skills. It's more than just offering feedback or book recommendations. Passive, ad hoc "development" won't take a team from great to elite. That requires active development of every team member.

You can do this during a one-on-one every week. These are 30-minute meetings between you and each of your direct reports. It's where you can have open discussions about challenges they're facing and help them blast through any barriers. But it's more than just getting a pulse on what's going on.

It's important to make the space to understand professional ambitions. This ensures what they are working on aligns with that direction. Plus, it builds rapport.

Develop Each Individual on the Team

Elite teams are great at their jobs *and* get better every month.

You already know each individual's dream of career success. They're already getting better because they're passionate about it and show a natural inclination. An individual skill development plan pours gasoline on that fire.

During the first one-on-one of each month, identify one critical area to develop. As with your company, focus on one area that will accelerate growth.

If they don't know where to get started, help them uncover the right opportunity:

1. How did you do last month qualitatively? What do you think you can improve on?
2. Here are the metrics for last month. What do you see across your metrics and targets?
3. What skill do you need to work on this month? What's the best way I can help you?

Once you identify what to develop for each direct report, identify one resource to help them develop in that area.

Identify One High-Impact Resource

The resource could be a book, a course, or a certification. The type of resource doesn't matter as long as it's effective training.

Ideally, the individual should identify this resource, as they'll be more motivated to engage with training that genuinely interests them. However, if you have a proven resource, recommend it. The value of this step is identifying a resource for them to use, which gives you a clear "done, not done" verdict at the end of the month.

If it's an area you both need to develop, do it together. For instance, when writing this book, Laura, our Director of Content, and I took the course Write Useful Books together, which helped us gain valuable skills. But hey, we'll leave it up to you—did it work? Is this book actually useful?

Once you've got your resource, coach them throughout the process.

Employee Performance Dashboard

Company Name: | Designed by: | Date:

Team Member

Audit | **Incentivize** | **Develop**

Core Values			
Frequency			

Job(s)	Motivation	Results	Skills	Capacity

Individual Incentive(s)

Team Incentive(s)

Top Skill(s) to Develop

Top Resource(s)

Download a virtual copy here

Based on the book The Product-Led Playbook: How to Unlock Self-Serve Revenue and Dominate Your Market (With a Tiny Team)

ProductLed®
productled.com

Support Them to Develop This Skill

At every weekly one-on-one with your direct report, ask them how the training is going. This acts as an important trigger to prioritize the training and shows that you're taking their skill development seriously.

If you have advanced skills in the training topic, coach them on how to improve by giving some examples of how they can master it. This alone is extremely valuable and accelerates skill development faster than anything else.

To boost accountability, make completion of these high-impact resources a personal project for employees, decide them in MFMs, and review progress in WAMs.

Use the Employee Performance Dashboard to audit, incentivize, and develop each team member.

Action Tool: Free Employee Performance Dashboard Template

Get your free Employee Performance Dashboard at ProductLedPlaybook.com.

Download a
virtual copy here.

Forge Your Elite Team

Eventually, your product will be copied. So will your marketing. So will your experience. Your long-term differentiator is your team—and how you improve it.

Even as other companies try to poach your talent, they won't be able to poach the elite, high-performance culture that cultivates it.

Actionable Takeaways

- You can afford to hire as a last resort when building a product-led business. Your product will solve most of your problems.
- When you invest in your team, you can get an insane return. Think of each employee as a stock you invest in. The only difference is you control how much it appreciates over time. If you invest more, you will get better returns.
- To free up your time, implement the 3T's by Trimming jobs that don't require your full expertise; Trashing jobs that don't contribute value; and Treasuring jobs that deserve your full time and focus.
- To audit your team, start with a quick audit to analyze if someone embodies the core values of your business. Then, complete a performance audit to analyze each job based on Motivation, Skill, Results, and Capacity.
- To incentivize your team, understand each direct report's big vision for their life and help them get closer to that vision each day. Trim or remove jobs from their plate that don't align with their vision. Help them double down and build more skills around the jobs that align with their vision.
- Make sure there's something meaningful at stake for your team to achieve the endgame. The true test is whether you and your team would feel crushed if you don't complete the endgame. If your team is apathetic about the endgame, you need to find a better incentive.
- Identify one skill for each of your direct reports to develop every month. Don't overwhelm them with a bunch of skills. Coach them on how to improve in one area.

Outro

Execute The Product-Led Playbook

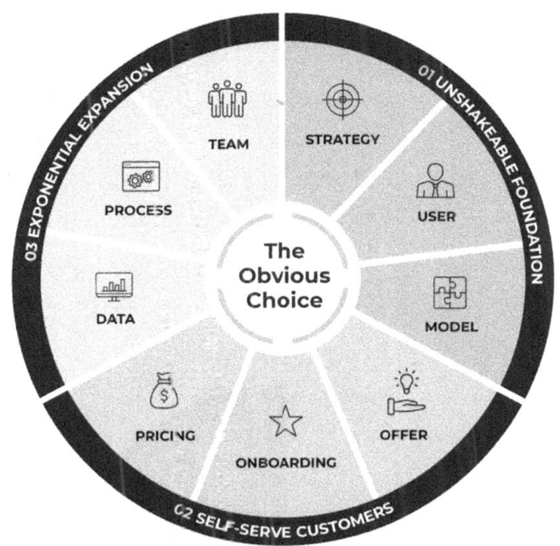

Installing the ProductLed System – A Simple Step-By-Step Roadmap

Surface-level PLG isn't going to cut it. Ninety-seven percent of buyers want to try before they buy. To succeed with PLG, you need to create the right environment for it to succeed.

It's not enough to just be good at PLG or have a good product-led organization. It's about integrating the two. Becoming product-led is how you make it happen.

The ProductLed System is your fastest, simplest way to do this.

With the nine components dialed in, you will **grow faster with less effort**. There's a strategic order to install the ProductLed System. Follow the roadmap laid out in this book:

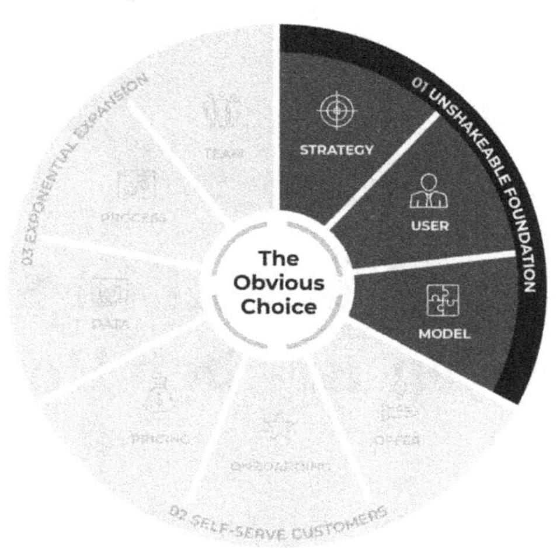

Stage 1

Build an Unshakeable Foundation

The goal is to transform your business from “scattered” to “streamlined.” You achieve that by rolling out these three components.

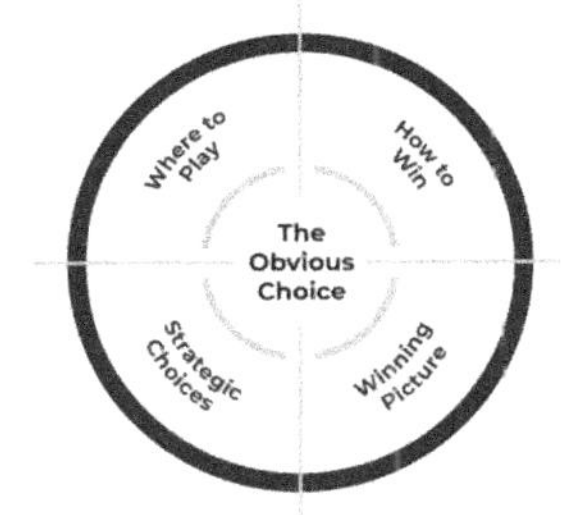

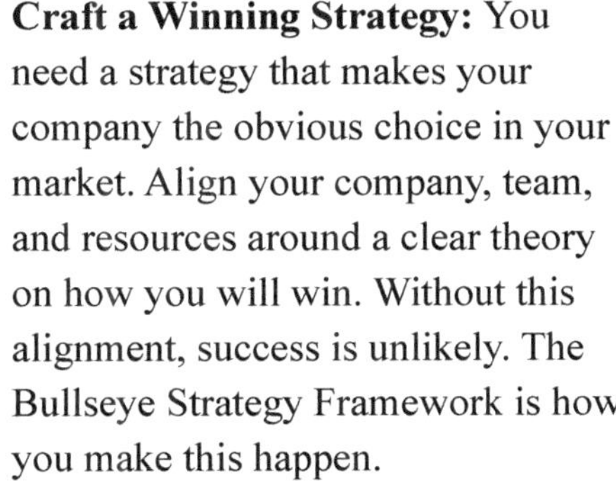

Craft a Winning Strategy: You need a strategy that makes your company the obvious choice in your market. Align your company, team, and resources around a clear theory on how you will win. Without this alignment, success is unlikely. The Bullseye Strategy Framework is how you make this happen.

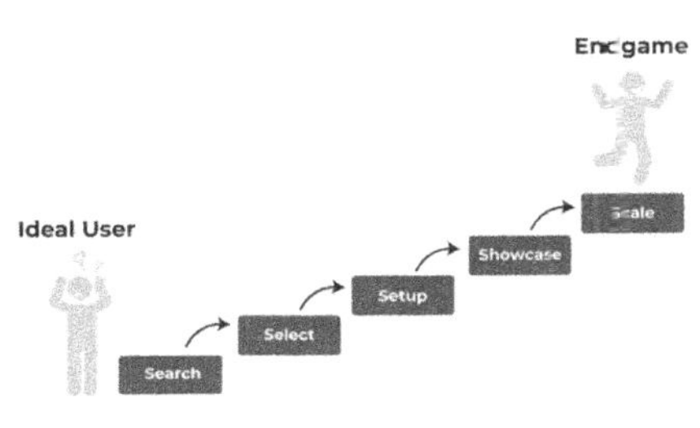

Identify Your Ideal User: After locking in your strategy, the next step is to understand your ideal user better than anyone else in your market. This deep understanding is crucial for creating an intentional model and irresistible offer. The User Endgame Roadmap Model will guide you through this process.

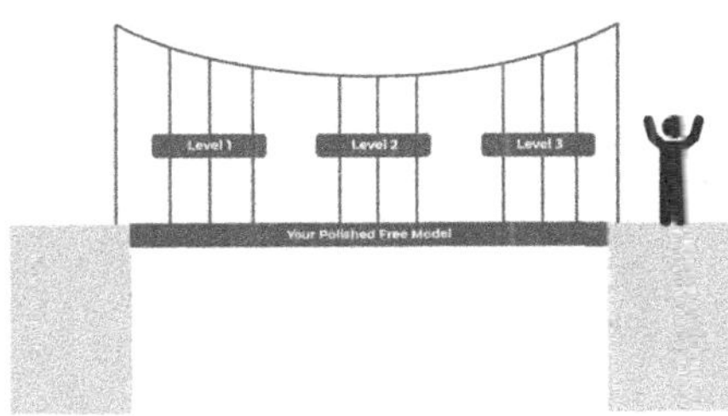

Design an Intentional Model: It doesn't matter what free model you use. What matters is identifying the challenges your users need to overcome to feel like they've reached the "next level" in your product and giving them everything they need to beat those challenges. The DEEP Model guides you through this.

Collectively, these three components give you the foundation you need to build a product-led business. If you skip one or do it in the wrong order, you risk building your business on a shaky foundation.

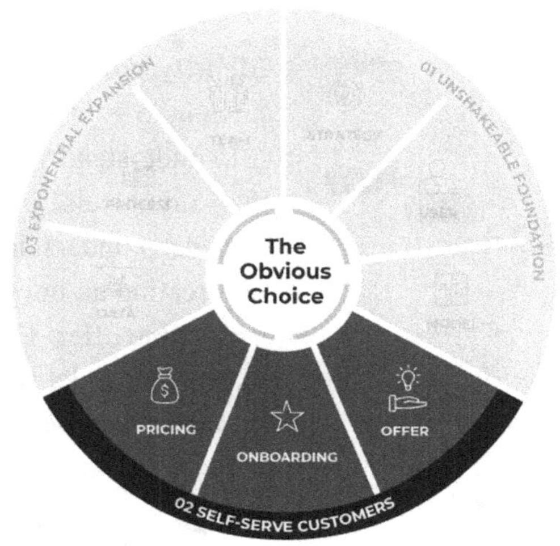

Stage 2
Unlock Self-Serve Customers

The goal is to shift from “high-touch” to “zero-touch” customers. This gives your business enormous leverage to scale—you don’t have to hand-hold each customer. The following three steps unlock self-serve customers.

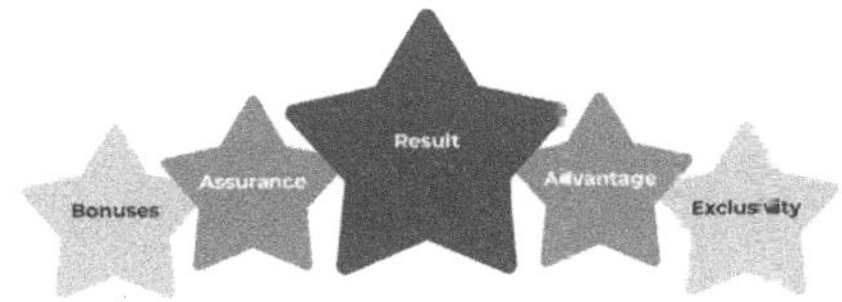

Build an Irresistible Offer: Your users are inundated with so many different solutions to solve their problems. You must have an irresistible offer that speaks to them and differentiates why your solution is the best. When you have an irresistible offer, you'll attract your ideal users and increase their motivation to use your product. The 5-Star Offer Generator is how you make this happen.

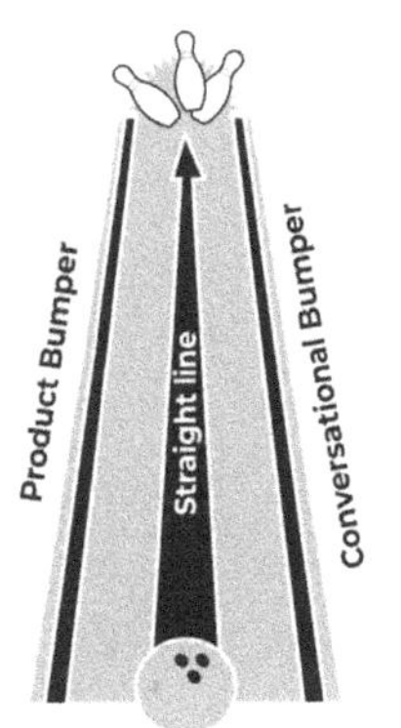

Design Frictionless Onboarding: Users need to experience the value of your product on their terms to feel confident purchasing it without a sales call. To get the majority of users to experience a First Strike, you must craft an experience that is effortless to sign up, get to value, and upgrade. The Bowling Alley Framework is how you do that.

Unlock Powerful Pricing: To turn users into high-paying customers, you must align your pricing with the value users receive when using your product. Without this win-win scenario, you'll aggravate users and kill your chances of automatically growing customer lifetime value. The Value Ladder Framework helps you achieve powerful pricing.

These three components help you unlock self-serve customers. Each one builds on the other, so don't skip ahead if this is your first time implementing the ProductLed System.

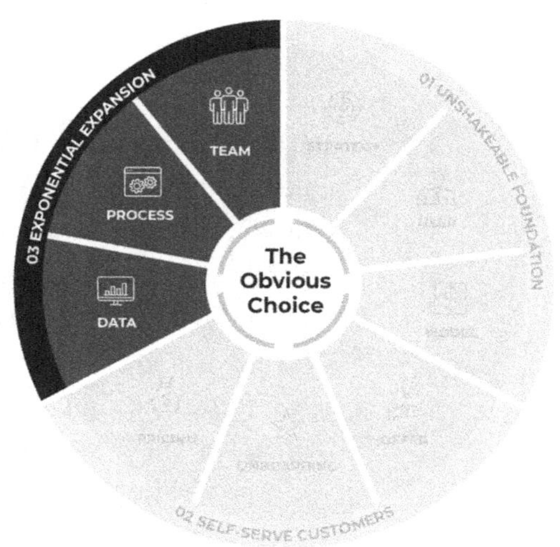

Stage 3
Ignite Exponential Expansion

The goal is to transform your business from "linear" to "leveraged" growth. You achieve that by rolling out these three components.

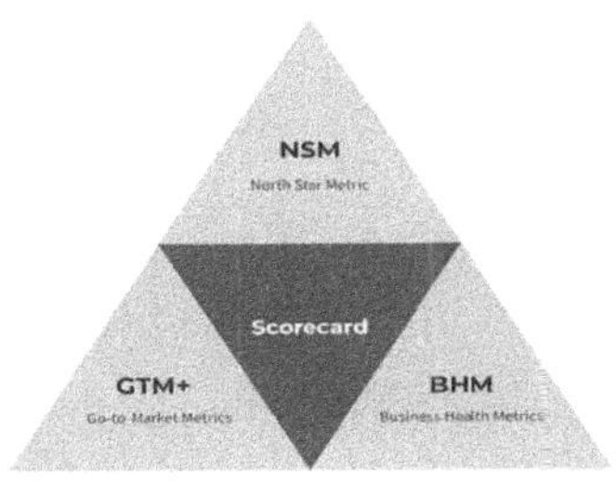

Access Actionable Data: Not all data is created equal. You must know what your #1 bottleneck is at all times. To do that, you need to build a ProductLed Scorecard and update it weekly to understand exactly what's happening in your business and where you should focus. The True North Framework helps you pinpoint those critical metrics.

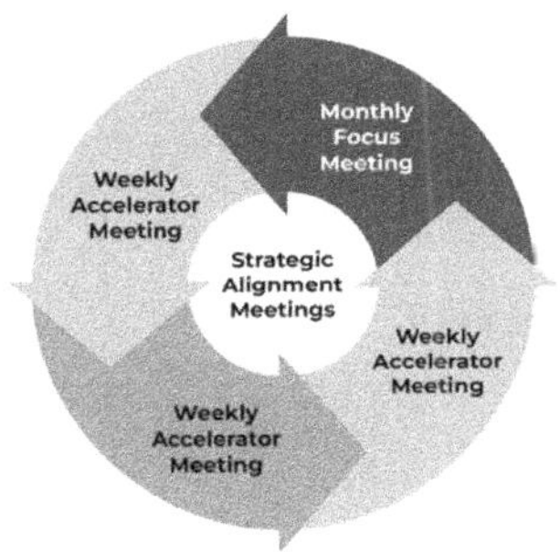

Adopt a Growth Process: You and your team need regular, structured meetings to stay aligned with your long-term vision and focused on your most important short-term projects. This discipline is key to achieving sustainable growth, which you can unlock by implementing the Predictable Growth Process.

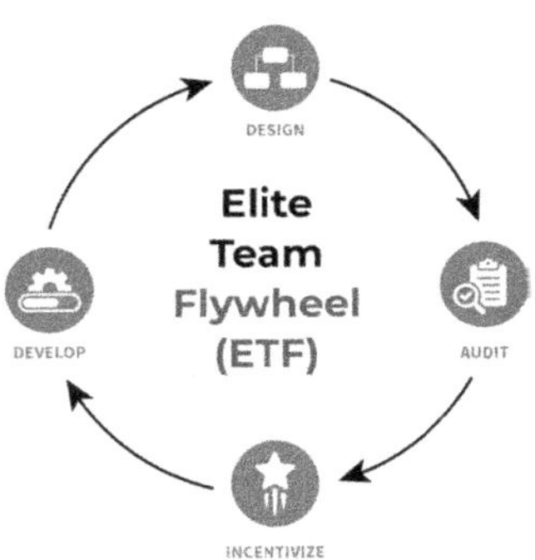

Build an Elite Team: Create an environment where your team consistently improves the skills they develop and the value they bring to your organization. To develop world-class capabilities, design a lean team, regularly audit their performance, incentivize what matters, and help them grow to their full potential. You can unpack this in the Elite Team Flywheel.

These tools will become essential to your daily operations, compounding your growth over time and positioning you as the obvious choice in your market.

Only the Paranoid Survive

What makes the ProductLed System unique is that it's a GTM-operating system—not a one-and-done effort. The minute you update any component, it starts to decay.

Your strategy is most relevant the day it's created. Your offer is most unique the day it's crafted. Your pricing is most powerful the day it's launched.

To stay at the cutting edge of your market, you must constantly update each component. At the very least, you should go through a full cycle of the ProductLed System once every year. For faster-growing companies, you might complete between 2 to 4 cycles annually.

Your GTM strategy needs to evolve based on market insights, changes in customer behavior, and the competition. It pays to be paranoid.

But let's put the paranoia aside for a second and unpack how to get the rest of your team on board to implement the ProductLed System with you.

Quick Start Action Plan

1) Educate Your Team on the ProductLed System

The whole premise of this book is that you must build a product-led organization that can support world-class PLG. To do that, your team must understand what the system is all about and the reasoning behind it. You want a team that can push back and debate with you on every one of these components.

To make it easier for your team to learn about the system, they can:

- Listen to *The ProductLed Playbook* for free on the ProductLed Podcast.
- Pick up a copy of *The ProductLed Playbook* on Amazon or wherever they can purchase a copy.
- Watch our free ProductLed Masterclass at ProductLedPlaybook.com. It's easy for you to share and align your team on what the ProductLed System is all about.

2) Benchmark Your Company

Implementing the ProductLed System will take some time. We created the ProductLed Assessment to assess your progress and learn which component(s) you need to dial in to scale faster.

By analyzing your business on the nine key components of the ProductLed System, you get a heatmap of your business's current strengths and weaknesses. You'll receive a free report that breaks down where you need to focus. The goal is to progress every 90 days, and your overall score should increase each time you complete the assessment.

The assessment should be taken multiple times throughout the year, but taking it now will serve as a benchmark for you to refer back to and see your progress over time.

 **Take Your Free ProductLed Assessment**

Benchmark your business in less than five minutes online at ProductLedPlaybook.com.

3) Personalized Game Plan

Once you complete the assessment, we'll help you scale your product-led business faster by offering you a complimentary one-hour growth call with one of our Senior ProductLed Implementers.

During this high-impact session, you'll craft a powerful, 30-day game plan that's focused on one core component of the ProductLed System that will have the biggest impact on your company's growth. This isn't just theory—it's a practical roadmap tailored to help you get momentum and start seeing results quickly.

This isn't a sales pitch. It's a genuine opportunity for us to better understand your business. If, at the end of our conversation, we believe we can significantly impact your growth, we'll show you how we help clients become the obvious choice in their market with the ProductLed Implementation Program.

In this program, you'll work closely with a ProductLed Implementer who becomes your strategic partner by offering the expertise, accountability, and execution power to bring your vision to life.

Let's start taking massive action today.

🎁 Claim Your Personalized Game Plan

Book a high-impact session with a Senior ProductLed Implementer at ProductLed.com/gameplan and create your 30-day game plan.

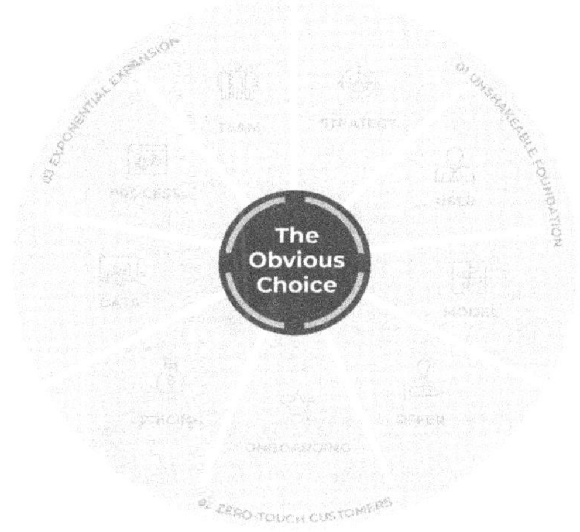

Will You Become the Obvious Choice?

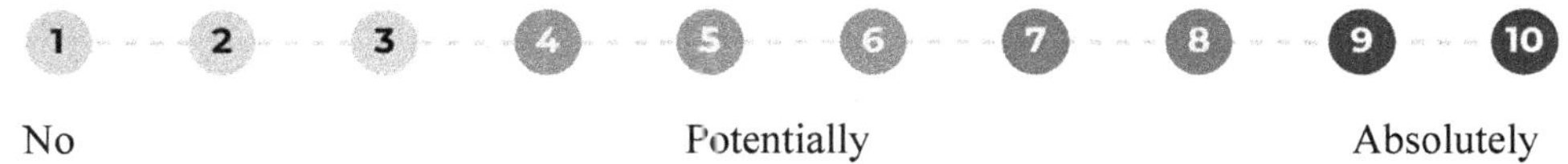

No Potentially Absolutely

Rate yourself from 1 to 10.

Odds are, you're in a competitive market. Everyone wants to steal your market share.

Creating a blue ocean strategy won't work for long. You need to thrive in a red ocean and become the obvious choice for buyers. *Now.*

There's only one obvious choice in every market:

One Zoom.
One Slack.
One Canva.
One HubSpot.

But here's what might surprise you: it's actually simpler to become the obvious choice than uprooting the current one.

Once you establish yourself as the obvious choice, your users automatically recommend your product over others, even if competitors eventually offer similar or slightly better products.

It might seem strange, but it's common—when people find a product they love, they stop searching for alternatives and stick with what they know.

Over the long run, this free advertising boosts profits, which gives you more gold to invest in making the best product and hiring top talent. This makes you harder to copy over time.

Geoffrey A. Moore covers this brilliantly in *Crossing the Chasm.* The book highlights how to cross the chasm from early adopters (who are willing to take risks on new technology) to the early majority (who are more cautious and pragmatic). To reach the next group of potential users, focus on getting your current users to recommend your product.

Obvious-choice products don't just cross the chasm faster. They win over the innovators, early adopters, late majority, and laggards. Laggards, in particular, are more risk-averse and just want to use what everyone else is already using.

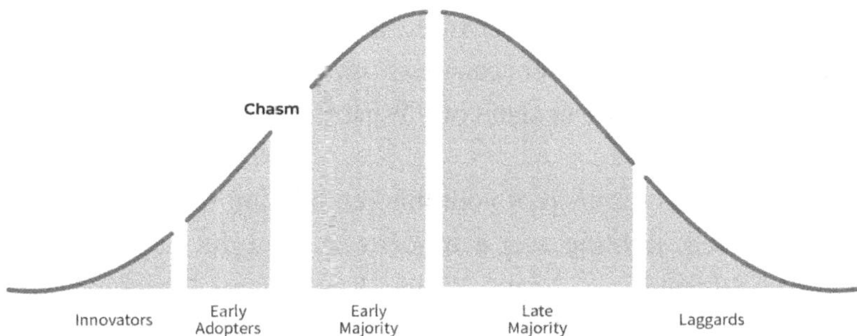

That's why there are jokes like "nobody gets fired for choosing Microsoft." Once you become the obvious choice, it's mind-numbingly hard for competitors to dislodge you from that position.

So the only question is, will you become the obvious choice *first*?

Predicting Your Future

If you look ahead into the next three years, you will end up in one of four circumstances.

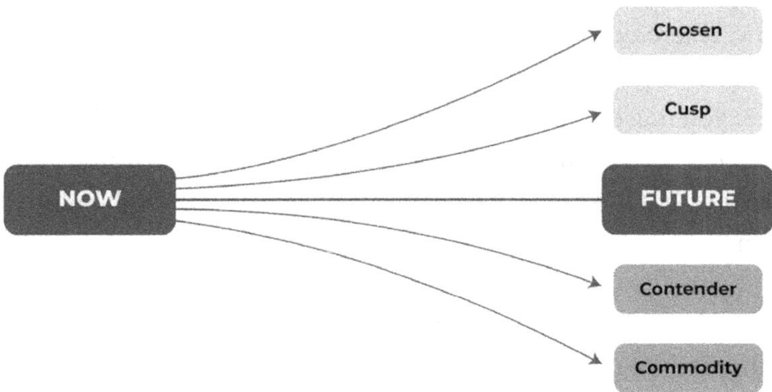

Commodity: You might be seen as just a Commodity in your market, where customers only choose your product if it's the cheapest. You're struggling to attract customers and make a profit. It feels like the game is rigged against you. How would it feel to be seen as a commodity a year from now?

Contender: You might find yourself being seen as just another player in your market. Most users don't know about you, but you offer something unique.

Contenders often get acquired for their unique features or copied by those already on top. Being a contender is tough because a unique approach isn't enough to protect your business—competitors can easily replicate what you do. You must gain meaningful market share to stand out. What would being a contender feel like?

Cusp: You could be on the cusp of your market, battling it out with a few tough competitors. You'd be fighting over a minority share of the market. As soon as you develop a new feature, competitors quickly copy you. As soon as you find a new marketing channel, competitors copy you. Because you lack sizable profits and are neck and neck with so many competitors, it feels like it's a constant fight to stay on the cusp. While the obvious choice is thinking long-term, you're stuck in the short-term, trying to outmaneuver the competition. What would being on the cusp of your market look like for you?

Chosen: You could reach the pinnacle of your market. You have become the obvious choice, and your market automatically refers to your product over any other solution. You take the lion's share of the market and enjoy automatic profits. Top talent is knocking at your door. What would becoming the obvious choice look like for you?

Which of these four circumstances best describes where you are at today? Be honest. Now, where do you *want* to be in the next three years?

To get there, you must do what's required. Moving up from one line to the next gets riskier, harder, and costlier as you progress. Many people think time is a straight line, but it's not. Time curves everything. Time is the ultimate compounding vehicle.

If you procrastinate and keep drifting along, there is no alternative other than to land in the Commodity zone. If you build an unshakeable foundation and implement Stage 1, your best bet is to become a Contender in your market. If you implement Stage 2 and unlock self-serve customers, you can gain the leverage you need to be on the Cusp of your market. It's not a bad place to be, but we both know you're capable of more.

To become the obvious choice, you must implement the entire ProductLed System and unlock exponential expansion. That's how you win.

When we work with clients, we do two things:

1. We help get you back on the fast path to becoming the obvious choice when you feel like you're drifting off.
2. We push the pace and bring accountability.

Some of our top-performing clients see a third, powerful opportunity: accelerating their growth by becoming a portfolio company of ProductLed. This strategic move not only speeds up results but also propels them to market dominance faster than they ever imagined.

That's a more intense level of working with us, and it's probably not the conversation for today. For now, the question is, "Do you want to become the obvious choice in your market?"

Your competitors might be reading this book—and putting it into action. Will they beat you to that top spot? Dislodging a competitor from there is mind-numbingly hard.

There's only room for one. And right now is your best shot to become the obvious choice in your market.

Thank You for Reading!

Congratulations on finishing the book!

I appreciate you choosing to spend your valuable time with me—it truly means a lot.

Now, I have a small request that can have a big impact: If this book helped you, would you take just 60 seconds to leave a review on Amazon?

Your feedback not only helps others discover how becoming product-led can transform their business, but it also supports me in spreading the word.

Here's how to leave a review in less than a minute:

Visit the book's page on Amazon (or wherever you purchased it) and leave a review directly on the page.

Thank you from the bottom of my heart.

Wes Bush

P.S. I'm eager to hear your thoughts on the book. Please send your honest feedback to wes@productled.com with "Review" in the subject line. Your input helps me grow as an author.

P.P.S. If you enjoyed this book, you'll also love *Product-Led Growth: How to Build a Product That Sells Itself* and *Product-Led Onboarding: How to Turn Users Into Lifelong Customers*. Both are available for free at ProductLed.com.

P.P.P.S. Want to help more companies successfully implement the ProductLed System? Learn more at ProductLed.com/Careers

About the Author

Wes Bush is a Canadian entrepreneur and author who pioneered Product-Led Growth (PLG). After seeing the power of PLG at Vidyard in 2016, he began consulting hypergrowth and Fortune 500 companies on PLG strategies. His bestselling book, *Product-Led Growth: How to Build a Product That Sells Itself*, popularized this approach and led to the creation of the ProductLed System™, a holistic approach to operationalize PLG within companies. Since 2017, ProductLed has helped 400+ companies generate more than $1 billion in self-serve revenue. Wes spends most of his time as a ProductLed Implementer, working hands-on with the leadership teams of SaaS companies to help them fully implement the ProductLed System™. Wes is on a mission to democratize product-led growth and enjoys traveling, triathlons, and reading history books.

Preview of *The Free Life*

I'm excited to share an exclusive preview of my next book, *The Free Life*. In this book, I'll dive deeper into how to design a business that serves you. I'll be sharing more on this topic as I refine my ideas at wesbush.com.

Escaping the Grind: Designing a Business That Serves You

Think back to when you first decided to start your business.

It wasn't because you wanted to work longer hours, feel more stressed, or constantly worry about cash flow. You started your entrepreneurial journey for something bigger: *freedom*.

Freedom to earn more.
Freedom to choose when and how you work.
Freedom to work from anywhere.
Freedom to do what you love.
Freedom to make a lasting impact.

But somewhere along the way, that vision may have gotten blurry. The long hours, the hustle, and the overwhelming pressure can make you lose sight of why you started in the first place.

The truth is, you deserve more.

You deserve a business that works for *you*, not the other way around—one that supports the life you dreamed of when you first set out on this path. A business that allows you to escape the grind and live on your terms.

It's about living your ideal entrepreneurial life—what I call "The Free Life."

This book walks you through how to create *The Free Life* in three transformative steps:

Step 1: Unleash Your Zone of Genius

As a founder, chances are you're spending over 50% of your time on tasks that don't tap into your Zone of Genius—the unique area where your natural talents, passion, and peak performance intersect. This is where you effortlessly excel and create the most value. In this step, you'll pinpoint your Zone of Genius and design an environment that empowers you to focus on what you're best at.

Imagine this:

- What if you could spend *all* your time doing what you truly love?
- What if your team was structured to handle everything outside your Zone of Genius, freeing you to focus on your unique strengths?
- What if the work that energizes you the most also drives the most significant results for your business?

By doubling down on your genius, you won't just be more productive—you'll build a business that thrives on your strengths, maximizing your passion and impact.

Step 2: Design Your Rich Life

A rich life isn't just about money. It's about creating a life that matches your values. It could mean paying yourself well, taking many vacations, working remotely, or enjoying a daily Starbucks latte. What matters is that it's fulfilling to you.

Imagine this:

- What if you no longer had to worry about money?
- What if you had the time to pursue hobbies, recharge, and truly enjoy the life you've designed?
- What if you had incredible *energy* and *health* to excel in your family, relationships, and business?

Designing your rich life means going from surviving to thriving. It's about more than financial success—it's about creating a life where your business supports your personal well-being, not just your bank account.

Step 3: Become Unstoppable

Success is great, but significance is what truly matters. To increase your impact, you must become more. This requires you to get crystal clear on the impact you want to have and acquire the skills and network to make that dream a reality. That's how you become unstoppable.
Imagine this:

- What if you had insane *clarity* on what ultimate success looks like in your life?
- What if you quickly acquired the *exact skills* you need to get to the next level in your life?
- What if you had a world-class *support system* to help you break through any barrier?

By becoming the best version of yourself, you unlock the ability to lead with purpose, tackle challenges with confidence, and create a lasting impact that goes beyond personal success.

Let's begin this journey together.

It's time to break free from the grind and start living **The Free Life**.

Acknowledgments

This book wouldn't have come to life without our trailblazing clients. You invested in implementing parts of this system long before it was fully polished. You ironed out the kinks and blazed the path for the rest of us to follow. You are the true heroes.

I owe a special thanks to my wife, Catherine. Your unwavering support through my early morning (4 a.m.) writing sessions made this book possible. Thank you for standing by me and helping me brainstorm a million different book ideas. I couldn't have done it without you.

A heartfelt thank you to Laura Kluz for co-developing this book with me. It has been a blast working together. Your patience is *truly* contagious—you never showed frustration, even when I asked for the 16th rewrite! You've managed our book creation team with brilliance.

To Missy Boscay, for bringing the visuals to life, and to Samuel Afolabi, for catching every typo—I appreciate all your hard work.

Simon Bowen, thank you for pushing me to refine my system and helping me identify my million-dollar promise: becoming the obvious choice in your market. Your insights took the ProductLed System from good to great.

Rob Fitzpatrick, your book and program on *Write Useful Books* challenged Laura and me to cut out everything unnecessary and keep things simple. Your guidance was invaluable.

To Gino Wickman, Mark O'Donnell, and EOS® Worldwide, thank you for paving the way in the business operating system space. You demonstrated the power of having a simple system to run a business, and many of your tools continue to play a vital role in the ProductLed System.

Now, I want to extend my gratitude to our subject matter experts. The ProductLed System is multi-disciplinary, and although I can now write confidently on each subject, I had a lot of help along the way.

Thank you, Roger L. Martin and A.G. Lafley, for your insights into building a winning strategy. Georgiana Laudi and Claire Suellentrop, your best practices on customer research were instrumental. Pedro Cortés, your approach to building high-converting landing pages laid the foundation for the Offer Component. Ramli John, your work on improving onboarding has been tireless and impactful. Greg Leach, thank you for being a sounding board for pricing strategies. Caleb Zimmermann, your leadership in running meetings at ProductLed has refined our growth process while teaching me countless best practices.

Sarah McVanel, thank you for coming in at the right moment and challenging me to strengthen the intro and outro. Your storytelling instincts helped shape the final structure of this book.

Finally, to everyone who played a part in bringing this book to life, whether mentioned by name or not—thank you. Your support and contributions have made this playbook possible.

Endnotes

1. Forrester. *Death of a B2B Salesman*. 2015. https://www.forrester.com/report/Death-Of-A-B2B-Salesman/RES122288.

2. Bush, Wes. "How do you prefer to buy a software product?" LinkedIn post, May 3, 2024. https://www.linkedin.com/posts/wesbush_would-love-your-help-with-a-stat-for-my-upcoming-activity-7192146920734167042-4Q4D

3. Bush, Wes. "How would you rate your freemium/free trial experiences?" LinkedIn post, July, 31, 2024. https://www.linkedin.com/posts/wesbush_most-free-saas-products-are-pointless-to-activity-7224401662470238208-fwqf/

4. ProductLed Index, 2023-2024. "How much self-serve revenue (SRR) did you generate last year?" Internal survey, based on data from 2,043 SaaS business.

5. ProductLed Index, 2023-2024. "What is your revenue per employee (RPE)?" Internal survey, based on data from 2,043 SaaS business.

6. ProductLed Index, 2023-2024. "What were your profits last year?" Internal survey, based on data from 2,043 SaaS business.

7. Statista Research Department, "Leading airlines in the U.S. based on passenger numbers 2023." May 28, 2024. https://www.statista.com/statistics/1109993/largest-airlines-north-america-passengers/#statisticContainer

8. Gallup. "Global Indicator: Organizational Culture." *Gallup*, 2024. https://www.gallup.com/471521/indicator-organizational-culture.aspx

9. Joyce, Nelson. "Moving From Free Trial to Freemium at Tettra: Two Years Later," *ProductLed* (blog), 20 October 2021, https://productled.com/freemium-business-model-example.

10. Department of Justice. "Justice Department Sues Live Nation-Ticketmaster for Monopolizing Markets Across the Live Concert Indsutry." May 23, 2024. https://www.justice.gov/opa/pr/justice-department-sues-live-nation-ticketmaster-monopolizing-markets-across-live-concert

11. Wes Bush, "How Product-Led Organizations Build Trust With Customers." *ProductLed* (blog), July 11, 2022. https://productled.com/blog/product-led-organization.

ProductLed Trademarked Terms

ProductLed System™

ProductLed®

Bullseye Strategy Framework™

User Endgame Roadmap™

DEEP Model Framework™

5-Star Offer Generator™

The Bowling Alley Framework™

Value Ladder Framework™

True North Framework™

Predictable Growth Process™

Elite Team Flywheel™

The One-Page Endgame™

ProductLed Implementer™

1-Year Picture™

Quarterly Picture™

Monthly Picture™

ProductLed Scorecard™

ProductLed Assessment™

Effortless ARR™

Lean Scale™

Durable Growth™

www.ingramcontent.com/pod-product-compliance
Lightning Source LLC
Chambersburg PA
CBHW060926210326
41597CB00042B/4512